Mountain hazards

By the same author

Mountain navigation techniques (1986)

Mountain hazards

Kevin Walker

Constable London

First published in Great Britain 1988
by Constable and Company Limited
10 Orange Street London WC2H 7EG
Copyright © 1988 by Kevin Walker
Set in Linotron Times 9pt by
Rowland Phototypesetting Limited
Bury St Edmunds, Suffolk
Printed in Great Britain by
The Bath Press Limited, Avon

British Library CIP data
Walker, Kevin
Mountain hazards,
1. Mountaineering – Safety measures
I. Title
363.1'4   GV200.18

ISBN 0 09 467900 2   796.522

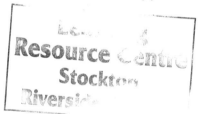

To Kelly Megan

'To become a mountaineer one must not only learn to climb; one must also learn to understand mountains.'

Gaston Rebuffat

Contents

Illustrations

(All photographs by Kevin Walker except those on pages 199 and 225 taken by Jeff Thomas)

Diagrams

(Diagrams drawn by Kevin Walker)

Acknowledgements

This book could not have been written without the help of many people. In particular I would like to thank John Inns and Jeff Thomas at Crickhowell Adventure Gear for their expert advice about equipment and clothing. John deserves special thanks for painstakingly reading the first draft and scribbling a number of constructive comments, whilst Jeff adopted a variety of strange poses in an attempt to model for some of the photographs.

I must also mention my wife, Lesley, who not only gave birth to our beautiful baby daughter, Kelly Megan, whilst I was struggling with the first draft, but also put up with me working until the early hours for weeks on end in order to finish the book on schedule. I failed dismally, so I must also thank my publishers for giving me those few extra weeks!

Finally I have to thank all those people with whom I have spent time on the hill, for without such experiences and camaraderie there would have been no book.

Introduction

This book is neither a catalogue of disasters, nor a 'survival book' in the modern sense of the word. It is more concerned with that indefinable skill which some call 'mountaincraft', and with the simple enjoyment of time spent in the mountains – whether walking, scrambling, or rock climbing.

Although entitled 'Mountain hazards', the book is more about the avoidance of such hazards than about the procedures to follow if they are met. I have always thought that preventative medicine is far superior to the treatment of symptoms. That being said, there are sections in which various 'treatments', so to speak, are discussed: for example, in addition to describing the causes and avoidance of mountain hypothermia, I have included suggestions about how to treat the condition if it is met on the hill.

In this context the term 'suggestions' is very important. Although many will no doubt see this as an instructional book, I would not presume to tell anyone what they can or cannot do whilst in the mountains. Following my book on mountain navigation techniques, this volume is the result of almost ten years' experience of running mountain activities courses and I have tried to answer those questions most frequently asked and to indicate ways of avoiding some of the pitfalls which are met by novices.

It is important you realize that reading this book alone will not make you a competent mountaineer or hill walker. Mountaincraft is a skill which relies heavily on past experience and sound judgement, neither of which can be taught. In addition, the constraints of space have made it impossible to go into every subject in depth and where necessary I have directed your attention to sources of further information.

For the sake of convenience I have divided the book into a number of parts. These divisions are fairly arbitrary and were chosen mainly in the hope that they would make the book easier to consult. Although some of the sections overlap, I have tried to avoid repetition by using cross-references wherever possible. In practice, life is not so categorized, and many of the hazards and conditions described will be met in combination with one another.

It is the ability to deal with these combinations and to recognize their inherent risks that I believe to be the hallmark of good mountaincraft.

The first part of the book deals with general aspects of mountain safety including footwear and clothing, food and equipment, attitudes, and planning. It briefly mentions various factors which should be considered when camping in wild country and then discusses the procedures which should be followed in the event of an accident.

In Part two we are concerned with the types of weather conditions which can be met on the hill. A gentle, moist breeze in the valleys can mean gusting winds and driving mist or rain at relatively minor altitudes, similarly the white fluffy snow in your back garden bears little resemblance to the various types of snow and ice which coat the mountains.

Part three deals with a number of human conditions such as hypothermia, heat exhaustion, and frost-bite. Although I have mentioned ways in which each of these ailments can be treated, they are all avoidable and I have tried to describe their causes in such a way that you need never suffer from them. A variety of minor disorders are also mentioned, and there is a brief discussion about the principles of basic mountaineering first aid.

Part four looks at mountain conditions, including avalanche, rockfall, and the problems posed by steep ground. Many of these hazards can be described as 'objective dangers' – problems which cannot be totally controlled. However, by approaching each problem in the correct way, armed with the knowledge that it is there, its inherent risks can be minimized.

This book is not supposed to negate hazards or risks, but simply to point out where they lie, for I have always believed that their recognition and successful avoidance is an important part of the enjoyment of the hills. Without the hazards and the risks, there would be no enjoyment, no reason to do friendly battle with rockface and ridge, no point in pushing ourselves to greater goals and greater achievements. If one were able to make the mountains safe, the overwhelming sense of adventure would be lost.

In all good adventure there is an element of risk. The greater the risk, the greater the skill required to overcome it, and the greater the adventure.

Part one

General mountain safety

1.1 Introduction

You may wonder why a book about mountain hazards starts with a section on general mountain safety. The justification is simple; I have always believed that the biggest hazard on the hill is the person who does not know, has not considered, or cannot be bothered to find out the basic principles of mountain safety. The 'I'm all right, Jack' or 'It'll never happen to me' attitude is not merely dangerous to the person concerned, but in this sphere perhaps more so than in any other, it can also prove hazardous to his companions.

One of the main attractions of all forms of mountain activities is the lack of rules and regulations. Long may it remain so! However, there are various principles of mountain safety that should be considered by anyone who wishes to wander in the hills, for whatever the reason. This part of the book is concerned with those principles.

Most books on mountain activities have a section discussing clothing and footwear, but although many tell you what you should wear, few tell you why. I have tried to illustrate the reasons behind the choice, for I am certain it is of the utmost importance that people understand why recommendations are being made rather than blindly following a list of someone else's preferences.

I clearly remember listening to a heated argument in the garden of a Lakeland pub one summer evening. A party of young people, most of whom had an air about them suggesting they were on their first mountain walking trip, were discussing the relative merits of socks. One young walker insisted that only one pair of loopstitch socks should be worn when mountain walking, whereas another was most emphatic that two pairs were the minimum. They both referred to the books which had told them that this was what a mountain walker *must* wear. At the time, I found this quite amusing, but it does have its more serious side. Both people were blindly following someone else's preference when, in all honesty, it

does not really matter how many pairs of socks you wear so long as your feet are comfortable and the socks are effectively doing the job for which they were designed.

I have also mentioned attitudes, and planning and preparation, for these play an important part not only in mountain safety, but also in the general enjoyment of the hills. Anyone who goes into the mountains without a certain amount of respect for their surroundings is undoubtedly asking for trouble.

Finally, no discussion of mountain safety would be complete without a brief summary of the procedures which should be followed in the unfortunate event of you being involved in, or coming across an accident on the hill.

1.2 Attitude

Mountain activities can be exhilarating. There is little to compare with the sight of a summer sunrise from the summit of a rocky peak climbed by moonlight, or with the tuneful silence of a sparkling, ice-festooned ridge in winter. These activities can also be gruelling and frustrating, and any exhilaration can soon be lost when the weather closes in or something goes wrong.

It is an unfortunate fact that people are needlessly killed and injured in the mountains every year. Even though rock climbing and mountain walking are activities involving a certain amount of risk, by far the vast majority of accidents are avoidable, being caused by ignorance, inexperience and sheer stupidity. Indeed, it can be argued that the underlying cause of most mountain accidents is a lack of appreciation of the risks, whether by ignorance, or by having the wrong attitude.

People take part in mountain activities for a wide variety of reasons. Some go in search of peace and tranquillity, some to prove themselves physically or mentally, others to do friendly battle with the mountain and themselves. The list is endless and defies analysis. On any summer weekend, in any popular mountain area in Britain,

The Bristly Ridge of Glyder Fawr in late Spring. If bad weather catches you in such terrain, you cannot simply walk away.

one can watch literally hundreds of people taking to the hills. There will be individuals, families, small groups of friends, and large parties from centres and clubs. What most of these people have in common is that they are visiting the mountains for enjoyment of one kind or another. What all the experienced mountain-goers amongst them have in common is an attitude: they all have a deep respect for the hills.

A mountain is an alien environment to most people, one which does not suffer fools gladly. Whilst never actually hostile, it is certainly indifferent to human suffering. If, for example, you are half way up a ridge and the weather turns bad, you cannot simply walk away. Like it or not, you are there, and have to cope with whatever problems come your way.

It can be argued that you should not have been caught out in the first place, either because of the local weather forecast (which you collected before you set off that morning), or because you recognized the cloud types and knew that they signified the approach of bad weather. Unfortunately, this argument does not take human nature into consideration and if you are at all enthusiastic about mountain activities, there will eventually come a time when you get into a situation where you have to choose between turning back or pushing on regardless. There is no doubt that this can be an extremely difficult decision, especially if you can only visit the mountains on a few weekends each year.

There is an unfortunate paradox here, for those people who are able to visit the mountains regularly are far more likely to turn back and visit the local hostelry than those who only have limited time available. And yet, generally speaking, it is precisely those people who visit the mountains regularly who are better equipped, both mentally and physically, to cope with adverse conditions. This is not an elitist attitude – it is simply a product of experience and judgement.

Do not fall into the trap of overestimating either your own ability, or that of your companions, because situations can easily get out of hand. For example, if you are three hours into a walk and stumble awkwardly breaking your ankle, you cannot simply pick up a telephone and ask for an ambulance. It could well be eight hours or more before a mountain rescue team can reach you and during that time you are going to be extremely uncomfortable, to say the least. Darkness may fall and the weather could easily take a turn for the worse. In addition, you will obviously be fairly inanimate, probably in pain and suffering from shock. The longer you stay on the mountain in these conditions, the greater the likelihood that you will fall victim to hypothermia.

One of the clearest examples of the importance of attitude is the fact that the majority of rock climbing accidents happen on the way down – having reached the top of the crag, it is all too easy to relax and lose your concentration. A similar thing happens in mountain walking, although not quite to so great an extent. Try to guard against becoming hasty and careless, and remember that the day does not finish when you reach your objective, but when you arrive back home. Remember also that problems caused by lack of concentration will be compounded by fatigue.

Once you set foot on a mountain you are committed – there is no easy way out. You have a responsibility to yourself and to your companions, and your attitude should reflect this commitment and responsibility. Nevertheless, if you are so preoccupied with identifying hazards that it destroys your enjoyment, there is little point in visiting the hills in the first place.

1.3 Planning and preparation

Assuming you have limited time, there is obviously little point in arriving at your destination not knowing what you want to do, or discovering on arrival that there is a tent pole missing. Many people would argue that careful planning and preparation can make all the difference between success or failure whether you are embarking on a major expedition or an afternoon stroll.

PLANNING
Try not to be in too much of a hurry to do the 'big routes' – they are not going to disappear overnight and you will undoubtedly enjoy them far more when you have the experience and expertise to tackle them confidently. Mountains tend to be unforgiving and you are

asking for trouble if you try to attempt too much too soon.

Different people have different ideas about how to plan a mountain walk when in an unfamiliar area. Many spend hours poring over maps; others simply pick up a guidebook and follow the author's chosen route. Assuming you have a reliable guidebook, this latter method is often a good way to get to know a new area, certainly in the early stages of your mountain walking 'career'. However, it does tend to be somewhat restrictive, and most people will want to graduate to planning their own routes, certainly once they have got to know their capabilities. You will also find that planning a route from the map gives you a better appreciation of the area as a whole – an important consideration should anything go wrong – and probably a greater feeling of satisfaction when you relax after having had a successful and enjoyable day.

When planning your route there are a number of factors which you should take into account. These include the time of year (mountain days are very short in winter, especially in Scotland), the type of terrain, how much equipment you will be carrying (i.e. will you be camping on the hill or is it just a day walk?) and the weather forecast. Although you should always plan with due regard for the prevailing conditions, do not forget that the weather can change remarkably quickly and that unforseen events can make a mockery of your time estimates. In addition, the terrain can change dramatically according to the seasons – the well-defined path which you followed in summer may well be hidden beneath a coating of snow and ice during the winter months.

You should also consider the size of the party and the experience and fitness of the individual members. If you are a group leader and are intending to go anywhere other than the valley floors, you should not be planning to take more than about six people with you. Larger groups tend to be unwieldy, and it can be argued that potential problems increase in direct proportion to the size of the group. It is impossible for one leader, however experienced, to keep tabs on every member of a group of twenty people, especially in misty conditions. Three is often considered to be the minimum number for a group; if someone has an accident, one person can stay with the casualty whilst the other goes for help.

When in the mountains the shortest route is rarely the easiest or quickest. One of the major principles of mountaincraft is to conserve energy, therefore you should avoid losing or gaining height unnecessarily. It is pointless toiling up and then down a short steep spur when it would be just as quick to contour around it, unless of course, there is something en route which you want to see. The detour may be slightly further, but it will usually be considerably easier and use far less energy.

The best time to plan a day's walk is the evening before you intend to go. You will then have access to up-to-date information on the weather and the state of the party, and when it comes to doing the walk the following day everything will be fresh in your mind.

It is a good idea – especially when planning to cross unfamiliar terrain – to make out a route card. Not only can this be used as an aid to mountain safety (a duplicate card being left with someone responsible), but it can also form an extremely useful reference document whilst you are on the hill, especially if the weather starts to deteriorate. There is a further advantage; in order to make an accurate route card you will have to study the map in a fair amount of detail, and the information so gained will give you a good idea of the general topography of the area – extremely useful in an emergency. An example of a route card is shown in Fig. 1, and full details of their construction, along with discussions on planning, timing, and route selection, can be found in my book, *Mountain navigation techniques*, also published by Constable.

Some people consider that route cards represent an unnecessary and unwelcome restriction. They argue that by leaving a route description with someone, they have to follow that route to the letter, thus denying themselves the freedom to stray wherever their fancy takes them. I have to admit that I do have a certain amount of sympathy with their point of view, but I consider it foolish to go into the mountains without leaving some word of where I am going. Philosophical considerations aside, there is no doubt that route cards have an important part to play, and that both novice parties and solo walkers should always leave a route card of some description with a responsible person.

Please note that if you do leave a route card with someone, it is

DATE :			START POINT:			
FEATURE	GRID. REF.	MAGNETIC BEARING	DISTANCE	HEIGHT CLIMBED.	ESTIMATED TIME	REMARKS

Front of card

Back of card

SIZE OF PARTY:

ESTIMATED TIME OF RETURN:

ESCAPE ROUTES:

OTHER RELEVANT INFORMATION:

Fig. 1. Example of a route card

extremely important that you let them know when you return. Try to imagine how you would feel if you were dragged away from a warm fire and good company on a Saturday night in order to look for an overdue party, only to find that they were safely ensconced in a local hostelry having neglected to tell anyone that they were back. There is no excuse for such inconsiderate behaviour.

Although the above remarks apply primarily to mountain walking, rock climbers who intend to visit the more remote mountain crags may find them useful. The advantage of having some form of guidebook when visiting an unfamiliar cliff should be obvious, as should the advisability of leaving word of where you have gone.

PREPARATION

Once you have planned your day you have to prepare for it. As with planning many experienced mountain enthusiasts tend to do this almost automatically, but it is a good idea to get yourself into the habit from the outset.

There are a number of ways to look at preparation. In overall terms, you should prepare yourself for mountain activities by making sure you are both physically and mentally fit to take part. This tends to be a long-term preparation and, generally speaking, if you are at all interested in mountain activities, you will also be reasonably interested in keeping your body in trim. If not, you should be! In any case, in the early stages of your mountain walking life you should not be going into the mountains alone, and you have a responsibility to the people you are with as well as to yourself. If you are unfit, not only might you hold them up, but you are also more likely to have (or cause) an accident. You may well be putting their lives at risk as well as your own.

In more immediate terms, it is a good idea to work out some form of routine whereby you prepare for each trip. There will be certain items of equipment and clothing that you should take with you. These will be described in detail in sections 1.4 and 1.5. Those which you will need on every journey into the mountains can be left permanently in your rucksack, (e.g. survival bag, emergency rations, small first aid kit).

When getting your kit and clothing ready, especially if you have not been on the hill for some time, you should carefully check everything to make sure that it is serviceable and will do the job for which it was designed. It is no good wearing a pair of boots whose soles fall off fives miles from the nearest road. Nor is there any point taking a gas stove with you only to find that, when you need it, the cylinder is virtually empty. To take it one stage further, there is little point in taking a stove and sufficient fuel if you have nothing with which to light it. The standard jokes, of course, are remembering the tins of food but forgetting the tin opener, or taking climbing harnesses but forgetting the rope!

Preparation extends from equipment and clothing to oneself. Even assuming you are fit, you still need to prepare your body, especially if your planned activity is at all ambitious. Whilst there is nothing to stop you visiting the local hostelry the night before a trip (and mountain enthusiasts being what they are, hostelries often tend to figure fairly prominently in the planning and preparation stages), you should aim to have a good night's sleep and to wake, without a hangover, ready to eat a large fried breakfast before sorting out food and drink and getting an update on the weather forecast.

In its widest possible sense, preparation means being equipped for any eventuality. Before you set off for the hill ask youself whether you could survive an unexpected night in the open. Do not forget, however, that weight is your enemy; there is no point in carrying useless items with you for they simply use up extra energy. Only experience will tell you what you need and what you can discard.

1.4 Clothing and footwear

Imagine getting caught in the rain during a Sunday afternoon stroll when you are half an hour away from your car. It can be a miserable experience. Even in summer you can get surprisingly cold, especially if there is a breeze, however slight it may be.

Now try to imagine the same situation but on a mountain, three hours away from the nearest road. The breeze has become a strong wind, the temperature has plummeted, the drizzle has become driving rain and sleet, and in a matter of minutes, the visibility has become so poor that you can hardly see your companions, let alone where you are going. Conditions like these can be met regularly in every mountain region in Britain during the *summer* months.

Whenever you go into the mountains, it is vitally important that you wear suitable clothing and especially suitable footwear, because you will be relying on your feet to move you from place to place. The problem is that there is no such thing as the ideal clothing or the perfect boot. Not only will there be a variation in requirements from person to person, but also, because mountains tend to make their own weather and to change it fairly rapidly, conditions and requirements may vary from hour to hour. The clothing you wear may have to protect the body from a wide variety of weather conditions during the same walk. The conditions themselves will be discussed in detail in Part two. What we are concerned with in this section are the various ways in which the body can be protected from the effects of those conditions.

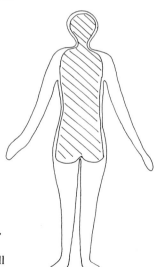

Fig. 2. The core and shell principle.
The shaded area represents
the core. The remainder is the shell

TEMPERATURE REGULATION

It will be helpful to think of humans as being creatures of two parts:
the *core* (containing the contents of the skull, chest and abdomen),
and the *shell* (comprising the rest of the body) (Fig. 2). Being
warm-blooded creatures, humans need to maintain a certain
temperature if they are to operate efficiently. If the temperature of
the core falls below a certain level, even if by only a small amount,
then the efficiency of the brain and the vital organs will begin to
deteriorate. If the temperature loss continues, it will inevitably lead
to coma and finally to death (See sections 3.2). Similar problems
occur if the core temperature increases (See section 3.3).

Even if the core temperature is maintained to within its limits,
large increases or decreases of temperature in or against the body
shell can lead to a variety of problems (See sections 3.4 and 3.6).

The main function of clothing is to maintain the temperature of
the core by regulating heat loss and heat gain. Due to the climate of
our mountains, it is the regulation of heat loss that is by far the more
important.

The body gains heat from a number of sources. Internal heat
production comes from the stored energy of food and from
muscular activity (including shivering), whilst external heat sources
include the sun, fire and hot food or drink.

There are five ways in which the body loses heat; conduction,
convection, evaporation, radiation and respiration.

Conduction is the transfer of heat between two objects which are
in contact. If, for example, you sit down on cold rock, you will begin
to lose heat. This loss is far more marked if your clothing is wet.
Indeed, if you are wet to the skin, your wet clothing will conduct
about two hundred and fifty times as much heat away from the body
than if your clothing was dry.

Convection is the cooling effect produced by the passage of air
over a warm surface. Unless there is an effective barrier between
the wind and the skin (or between the wind and any insulating
layers of clothing), there will be a marked loss of body heat through
convection.

Evaporation of sweat or climatic moisture (e.g. mist, rain, melted
snow, etc) which has dampened the clothing can result in

considerable heat loss if not controlled. Ventilation to reduce the amount of sweating is therefore fairly important, but one must be careful not to overventilate and increase heat loss through convection. It is also important to realize that sweating is a natural cooling mechanism, initiated by the body in response to overheating.

Radiation is the transfer of heat between the source (in this case the body) and the air, and is an important factor. For example, in still air at 5°C, an uncovered head can radiate up to fifty per cent of the body's heat production.

Finally, *respiration* cools. Although this is most noticeable at high altitude and during strenuous climbing when the heat loss can be considerable, evaporation of the water vapour in exhaled breath always leads to a slight heat loss.

In practice it is very difficult to separate these five functions because they tend to work hand in hand. To take a hypothetical example; imagine a person who has just reached a summit after having toiled up a steep mountainside in misty and slightly windy conditions. The muscular effort required by the climb has produced heat, and owing to a lack of ventilation, he has been sweating. This moisture has soaked the inner layers of his clothing. The moisture from the mist has soaked the outer layers, and the stronger gusts of wind pass through all his clothing and reach his skin. As it appeared to be quite warm when he set out from the valley, he thought it unnecessary to bring hat or gloves, a decision which he now regrets. In addition, he has decided that he is not as fit as he thought, and being out of breath has sat down on a convenient rock on the summit.

His heat loss will now be phenomenal. Radiation from his uncovered head will be high, as will the heat loss through respiration and through conduction into the cold rock on which he is sitting. His wet clothing will be acting in a number of ways. Evaporation and convection from the surface layers will be rapidly cooling the clothing, and this will increase the heat loss from the body due to conduction. In addition, gusts of wind will increase evaporation, and may remove the few patches of warm air which remain. As he is now tired and resting, heat production will be low.

General mountain safety   30

In this situation we must assume that heat loss greatly exceeds heat
gain. Unless this loss is checked, he will shortly become hypothermic
(See section 3.2). This is obviously not the way to do it.

THE LAYER SYSTEM
By wearing the correct clothing, it is possible to prevent most of the
heat loss described above. The problem is finding clothing (or
combinations of clothing) that will cope with the almost infinite
variety of wet, cold and windy conditions which can be met whilst in
the mountains. This problem is compounded by the fact that
mountain activities have become big business, and there is therefore
a bewildering amount of clothing available made from a confusing
array of different fabrics.

Whilst everyone has different tastes, and notwithstanding the fact
that there are a number of ways around the problem, the basic
principles remain the same. Clothing should be composed of a
series of insulating layers covered by a windproof outer layer. A
waterproof shell is also needed in order to keep these layers dry.
There should be no restriction of body movement or blood flow,
and there should be a good overlap at junctions (i.e. at the waist).
Protection of the extremities (head, hands and feet) completes the
picture.

The layer system is effective for two reasons. Firstly, air is an
extremely effective insulator and the more layers of clothing you
wear, the more layers of air you trap. Two thin sweaters are
therefore warmer than one thick sweater. Secondly, you can control
the amount of ventilation simply by removing or adding layers, thus
avoiding being always either too hot or too cold – a problem
commonly met by novices. A general rule, bearing the layer system
in mind, is that thickness equals warmth.
Insulating layers There are various materials which can be used in
the layer system. The best for the innermost layer is undoubtedly
polypropylene, as used in good quality thermal underwear. This
removes moisture from the skin leaving a dry layer next to the body,
thus helping to reduce heat loss through conduction. Wool is also
excellent, although many people find it unbearably itchy.

With regard to the middle layers, wool is undoubtedly the best of the natural materials because it retains much of its insulation even if it gets wet. Indeed, wet wool can actually give out heat due to a complicated chemical reaction. However, wool absorbs water and is heavy when wet; it takes a relatively long time to dry out, and is fairly bulky. Nylon fibre pile, polyester, acrylic and spun synthetic filaments are all weight-for-weight warmer than wool, retain their insulation properties when wet, and dry out quickly. They are also generally less bulky. Polyester and acrylic fabrics in particular absorb very little water.

Outer layers It is obviously of little use wearing a series of insulating layers if the first gust of wind cuts through them and removes all the warm air. Even if your layers are composed of one of the more wind-resistant insulating fabrics, you should wear (or at least carry) an outer windproof layer. The traditional garment is the anorak, a water-resistant jacket which is long enough to cover the buttocks. Most have storm cuffs, at least one map-sized pocket and a large hood. Some anoraks have full length zips and are worn like jackets, whilst others have only half length zips and must be put on over the head – a procedure which has attendant risks when standing on a narrow ledge in windy weather.

Similarly, it is pointless wearing your insulating layers if you get soaked to the skin every time it rains. In the past the vast majority anoraks were water-resistant as opposed to being totally waterproof, because a fully watertight shell causes body moisture to condense. Indeed, wearing a totally waterproof shell on a warm but misty day can result in getting wetter through condensation than you would through the mist! Traditionally therefore, a separate waterproof layer was carried, usually made from lightweight proofed nylon. The most common garment of this type was the cagoule, a three-quarter length, lightweight nylon 'sack' with arms and a hood.

Waterproofs are usually windproof. However, windproofs need not be totally waterproof. A waterproof garment can therefore serve two functions, albeit uncomfortably – for although you will get damp from condensation, the waterproof shell will prevent evaporation so there will only be a small amount of heat loss through conduction and convection.

Nowadays modern technology is coming to the rescue with breathable fabrics. These have revolutionized outdoor clothing to such an extent that it is no longer strictly necessary to separate windproofs and waterproofs. A breathable fabric is one which will allow water vapour to pass through, but not water droplets. There are various ways in which this can be done, some more successful than others. The idea is not entirely a modern one. Ventile, an extremely closely woven cotton fabric, has been available for decades. Possessing many of the attributes of the modern breathable fabrics (including high cost), some people would argue that it is considerably more durable.

The decision to have either separate windproof and waterproof garments or one dual-purpose garment will be largely a matter of personal choice. What is important is that you understand why such garments are needed. If you are unsure which to choose, a visit to a reputable mountaineering equipment shop will probably help. The good retailers know what they are talking about and will be able to show you a range of garments and explain the differences between them.

Design features which may be found useful in walking jackets or anoraks include wired hoods large enough to go over balaclavas or climbing helmets, large-toothed zip-fasteners (which neither jam nor freeze so easily as their small-toothed counterparts), internal map pockets accessible without having to undo the garment, velcro- or popper-closed baffles over the zips and/or pockets, internal storm-cuffs with adjustable elastic, taped seams, etc.

PROTECTION BELOW THE WAIST
So far we have concentrated on what to wear above the waist, but the same principles apply to the lower garments. Many people wear breeches and long socks (stockings) because they cause little restriction of leg movement. An added advantage is that the stockings can be rolled down and the bottoms of the legs left undone to give a pleasant amount of ventilation. There is nothing

Winter walking on Llangynidr moors. Note gaiters, windproof jackets, hat, mittens, and rucksacks.

wrong with trousers, but you will soon find they need to be fairly
loose fitting.

   Whatever you choose, the material from which they are made
should be wind resistant and fairly warm. Traditional materials
include woollen fabrics like tweed and moleskin, but modern
stretchable synthetic fabrics (which are windproof and dry quickly)
are becoming increasingly popular. Jeans are unsuitable for
mountain work as they are generally too restrictive and, more
importantly, have minimal insulation value when wet. For similar
reasons, it is inadvisable to wear cotton corduroy.

   In very cold conditions you will need extra layers, usually
comprising either thermal underwear (in the form of long johns) or
fibre-pile trousers. Even a pair of tights will make a substantial
difference. When wet and windy, a pair of overtrousers will help to
prevent heat loss, and whilst even good quality nylon overtrousers
tend to be hot and sweaty (many people try to avoid wearing them
for as long as possible), overtrousers in ventile and man-made
breathable fabrics are available (at a price) and are far more
pleasant to wear. These also have the added advantage that they
can be worn as windproofs on dry but blustery days.

ELIMINATION OF COLD SPOTS
One of the problems of wearing separate above- and below-waist
garments is that there is inevitably a cold spot between the two. One
way around this is to wear long upper garments; many shirts
designed specifically for mountaineering have extra-long tails.
Another way around the problem is to wear salopettes. These are
basically romper suits for adults and are available in both full-length
and knee-length styles.

PROTECTING THE EXTREMITIES
You will find that having a warm torso will help to keep the
extremities warm. This is simply a function of the blood flow
between the core and the shell. If the core temperature is
satisfactory, blood will flow freely to the shell, thus carrying warmth
to the extremities. If, however, there is an overall heat loss, the
capillaries will begin to constrict, reducing both the blood flow and

the heat loss. This process is known as *vaso-constriction*, and can be a contributory factor in frost-bite (See section 3.4).

Even if your torso is well protected, cold and wet and wind can combine to numb the hands and feet unless protected, and as has already been noted, substantial heat loss can occur from the head. A simple woolly hat will go a long way to reducing this latter heat loss, as will the increasingly popular 'Inca hats' with ear flaps. For really inclement conditions there is little to beat a balaclava. Traditional woollen ones are still very popular, but it is now possible to buy them made from polypropylene (thermal underwear material) and from various types of synthetic fleece. The more windproof they are, the better, although they will often be worn in conjunction with the hood on your outer layer. Avoid those paramilitary masks with separate holes for each eye; they tend to restrict the vision far too much.

If your balaclava is not long enough to tuck well into your shirt, a woollen scarf will help prevent both unpleasant drafts and the escape of warm air from around the neck. It has the added advantage of preventing rain from seeping in around the hood.

With regard to hands, mittens are undoubtedly warmer than gloves, although they can be cumbersome. If you need to use your hands to any great extent, fingerless gloves can be very useful. Also available are thin, thermal gloves which can, if necessary, be worn under mittens. In winter conditions you should have an inner thermal layer covered by an outer windproof shell. Ideally this outer shell will also be waterproof. In very cold conditions it is particularly important that there should be no restriction of circulation (See section 3.4).

INSULATED JACKETS
Mention must also be made of duvet jackets, those 'Michelin Man' parkas which used to be regarded as the trademark of the mountaineer. Now becoming commonplace, the versions available from high-street stores are usually more fashionable than functional. Even those designed specifically for mountain use come in several different styles with a variety of inner and outer materials and fillings.

   Few duvet jackets are one hundred per cent waterproof, and for this reason it is perhaps unwise to buy those with a down filling, for down loses all its insulation properties when wet. Down duvets with a breathable waterproof outer layer are available, at a price, but few people who buy them will want to stuff them into the bottom of a dirty rucksack! An alternative may be to treat ordinary down-filled duvet jackets with a total-immersion waterproofing compound. Generally speaking, however, those with a synthetic filling are far more functional and, despite what the technical specifications may tell you, the more bulky the filling, the warmer it feels. Admittedly, much of this may have to do with psychology.

PROTECTION IN HOT WEATHER
So far the assumption has been that you are going to meet cold, wet and windy conditions whenever you visit the hills. British weather being what it is, you will probably find that this is correct for much of the time. However, there will be occasions when the wind drops and the sun beats down, and you will want to strip off as many layers as possible. In these conditions, there is no reason why you should not wear shorts and a T-shirt, providing you carry extra clothing with you. This should include protection for the arms and legs, plus a lightweight and light-coloured cotton hat to give protection to the head and neck (See sections 3.3 and 3.6).

SOCKS AND STOCKINGS
Last but certainly not least, we come to the feet. Foot protection, by means of socks or stockings and boots, is extremely important and should not be underestimated. What would be regarded as a minor blister under normal circumstances can become a serious hazard on the mountains, where your only means of transport are your feet.
   Socks and stockings are far more important than you might at first think; as well as providing insulation, they should cushion the foot, reduce the amount of friction between it and the boot, and be able to absorb any perspiration. Wool is by far the best material for these purposes, and a loopstitch construction is generally regarded as being the most comfortable and effective. However, socks and stockings made from pure wool tend to wear out fairly quickly; a

ratio of 70 per cent wool : 30 per cent nylon is more durable, whilst still performing the essential functions. As with other garments, these should not restrict the circulation – you should be able to wriggle your toes with ease.

More rubbish has been written about the number of socks that should be worn than about almost any other mountaineering subject. It really does not matter whether you wear one, two, or even three pairs of socks, as long as your feet are comfortable and remain that way. Some people cannot bear to have wool next to the skin, in which case a thin pair of cotton under-socks will help. Other people need two or more pairs in order to cushion their feet from the considerable hammering which results from mountain walking. The only way to find out what is right for you is by trial and error; you may even find that when changing boots you need to change the number of socks you wear.

Whatever you eventually decide, you should keep your socks clean, washing them regularly. A fabric conditioner in the final rinse will help to keep them soft. You will find it is false economy to darn socks; however well they are repaired, they are more likely to cause blisters than undarned socks.

In addition to socks, insoles can be used to provide shock absorption or to give the boots a more comfortable fit. The best are those shaped to give support to the arches, and made of closed cell foam which does not absorb moisture, or sorbothane.

GAITERS
Gaiters are very useful as an extension of the layer system. Indeed, they should be regarded as essential in winter conditions. Nylon gaiters are the cheapest, but they are hot and sticky and tend to be noisy as you walk along. Most people prefer those made from canvas or cordura. Gaiters made from breathable fabrics are expensive and have the reputation of losing their breathable qualities fairly rapidly.

In addition to being windproof and waterproof (an occasional spray with a proofing compound will help), gaiters have the advantage of preventing foreign bodies from working their way into your boots. Yeti gaiters give added protection as they completely

enclose the boot leaving only the sole showing, whilst at the other
extreme are *stop tous* – tubes of nylon which fit around the top of
the boot.

BOOTS

Arguably the most important items you will ever need are boots.
Good sturdy boots are necessary for anything more than simple
low-level walks or short strolls along good paths. As with clothing,
there is no such thing as the ideal boot and most people have to
compromise. Nowadays, the more dedicated (or wealthier)
mountain enthusiasts buy two pairs – a pair of lightweight boots for
summer and a pair of more robust boots (often double boots with
plastic outers) for winter.

When choosing boots there are a number of things which should
be taken into consideration, one of the most important being the
stiffness of the sole. Although personal preference will play a large
part, there are some technical requirements as well. If you intend to
do any winter mountaineering, you will need a boot which is robust
enough to cope with step kicking, and stiff enough to take
crampons. Modern plastic boots would seem to fit the bill perfectly.
However, they are not really suitable for general mountain walking
in summer, when a lighter, more flexible boot is far superior.

A good compromise for general mountain walking is a
medium-height leather boot which, although fairly difficult to bend
by hand, will flex slightly across the ball of the foot when standing
on tiptoes. As with clothing, it is worth visiting a good
mountaineering shop so that you can see the range of footwear
available and get up-to-the-minute advice on the various models.
Whatever type of boot you choose, it should be as near a perfect fit
as possible, and for this reason you should never buy boots via mail
order.

When trying on boots in the shop, start with those of the same
size as your shoes, and progress upwards or downwards from there.
The most important consideration is comfort. They should be snug
without pinching, the toes should not reach the end, and the heel
should not move when you walk. A good quick check is that with
the boot laced and the foot pushed as far forward as possible, you

A typical selection of modern walking and mountaineering boots.

should just be able to get a finger between the back of the boot and your heel. You should, of course, wear the same number and thickness of socks as you intend to wear on the hill.

The type of sole is obviously of paramount importance, as is the method by which it is fastened to the rest of the boot. Most soles are either welded, screwed, sewn or glued to the upper, many boots have two or more of these methods used in combination. The welt (the projection of the sole around the boot) should be fairly narrow.

The sole itself should be either of the traditional pattern or the more recent monobloc type. Most people consider rubber to be far superior to PVC. Whatever the type it should have good frictional qualities and be thick enough to cushion the feet from sharp stones and pebbles. Although modern rubber soles are a vast improvement on nailed boots in the majority of situations, they do have some limitations of which you should be aware. They are, for example,

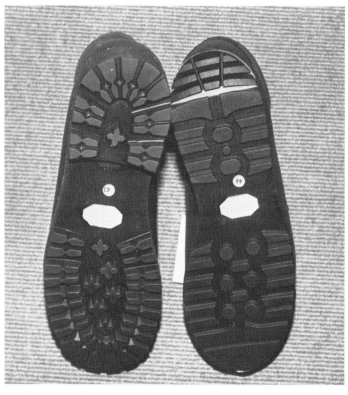

Traditional (*left*) and monobloc soles. Note the angled heel on the monobloc type.

notoriously slippery on very wet or very dry grass, greasy rock, hard snow, and ice.

In addition to stiffness along the sole, there should also be a high degree of stiffness across the sole (i.e. you should not be able to twist the boot width-ways), and the boot should be high enough to give reasonable support to the ankle, and sturdy enough to protect the heel and toes.

Other desirable features include a sewn-in or 'bellows' tongue, hook-and-eye lacing, and as few seams as possible. Not only are seams the weakest part of a boot, they also have a nasty habit of letting in water and for most practical purposes your boots should be as waterproof as possible. However, many people – myself included – prefer lightweight boots with fabric panels for general walking in summer and despite some manufacturers' claims, this type of boot is rarely waterproof. In the more expensive models, breathable waterproof fabrics have been used in an attempt to solve the problem but, to date, these have not been one hundred per cent successful. Padded socks made from the same material have also appeared on the market, but again, these have not met with much success. The main problem with using breathable fabrics for these purposes is their durability – they either keep their breathability and loses their waterproofness, or vice versa.

A good pair of leather boots will last for years if you look after them well. Apart from cleaning off the worst of the dirt after each walk and giving them a fairly regular dose of a specialist waterproofing wax, you should occasionally top up the natural oils in the leather with a conditioner. One of the most common mistakes is to treat the boots with too much liquid conditioner or dubbin. This results in the leather becoming so soft and supple that it literally cannot stand up to the wear and tear of mountain walking. The toes will become heavily scuffed and the seams will start to come apart not, as is commonly thought, due to the stitching rotting (most modern boots use synthetic thread), but because the leather has become so soft that the stitching has cut through it.

Another common error is attempting to dry wet boots too quickly. Leather does not like heat and unless it is left to dry naturally, it will stiffen and warp and, in severe cases, may even crack. The best way to dry boots is to stuff them with newspaper and leave them in a cool but airy room.

If you have just been introduced to mountain activities, do not let all this talk of specialist clothing and footwear dampen your sense of adventure and enthusiasm for what is essentially a very personal and 'basic' pastime. It is not necessary to go out and buy vast quantities of expensive clothing in order to enjoy the mountains. There is a lot to be said for starting out with basics and working up from there, for in this way you will appreciate what you need and why you need it, rather than relying on other people telling you what they think you need. However, the better clothed and equipped you are, the less you need worry about the weather. This can only be a good thing, for to enjoy the mountains at their best you will need to visit them in all conditions.

With all clothing and equipment you should buy the best you can afford, but you do not have to buy everything at once. Although it makes sense to start with a pair of boots (without boots you are not going to get very far), your first pair need not be expensive. Wait until you know exactly what you want before you start lashing out large amounts of money. After boots, you will probably find an anorak most useful, and by the time you are ready to buy the next large item, you should have done enough walking to know what you want.

1.5 Equipment and food

In the previous section I stated that it is unnecessary to buy vast quantities of expensive clothing in order to go safely into the mountains. Exactly the same applies to equipment.

I once came across two tired walkers near the summit of Bannau Brycheiniog, one of the peaks in the wild and remote area west of the Brecon Beacons. They were both carrying huge rucksacks and I automatically assumed that they were backpacking across the National Park. Enjoying the camaraderie of the hills (something which unfortunately seems to be on the wane), we struck up a conversation and I was astounded to discover that they were simply out for the day. Although the weather was superb and the forecast settled, they seemed to be equipped for almost any eventuality; they had so much gear that they could quite easily have set up a sizeable base camp complete with two large and somewhat heavy tents, sleeping bags, stove and dixies, and enough food, water and fuel to last a week. They even had an entrenching tool with which to dig an emergency latrine! Strangely, in spite of all this gear, either

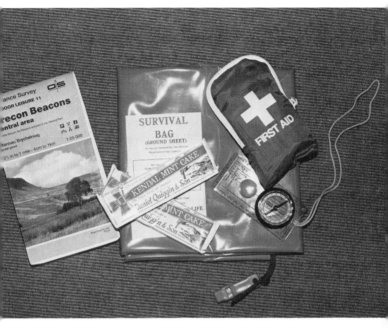

Essential items. Note map, compass, whistle, survival bag, first aid, and emergency food.

they had forgotten their first aid kit or it was at the bottom of one of their rucksacks, for they asked me if I could let them have something with which to relieve their blisters. Whilst it is obviously better to err on the side of caution, there are limits, and these two people had definitely gone over the top.

ESSENTIAL ITEMS
There are few really essential items of equipment. Admittedly there are certain things which, although not essential, are sometimes carried in order to make life a little more comfortable, but their usefulness is often tempered by their weight, and weight – as you

will soon discover – is one of your greatest enemies.

Assuming you are going with a group of people (and it would be wisest for you not to go walking alone in the high mountains until you are fairly experienced), there are quite a few things which can be shared. However, everyone should have their own map, compass and whistle, spare clothing, survival bag and emergency food. It is also wise for each person to have a small first aid kit.

Map and compass. It is pointless taking a map and compass anywhere unless you know how to use them, for they possess no magical properties of their own. Of the two, by far the most important is the map, and you should do your utmost to become skilled in map interpretation. The compass should be regarded as a secondary tool which can make life a little easier when the visibility begins to deteriorate. If you cannot interpret your map, you will find your compass is virtually useless. Full details can be found in my book, *Mountain navigation techniques*, also published by Constable.

Whistle. A whistle is an essential piece of safety equipment which should be used solely to signal distress. It should not be used as a musical instrument or be blown for fun. I once went to the rescue of a group who, having become separated in the mist, had given 'a few quick blasts' in order to join up again. Although, theoretically, you should never need to use your whistle for this reason (simply because you should never become separated from the group, no matter how bad the visibility becomes), it is probably better to get the group back together again by this means than it is to have to call out a rescue team later to look for one missing member.

Far worse was the time a colleague called out a mountain rescue team in atrocious conditions to go to the assistance of a group which appeared to be in serious difficulties as they were continuously blowing their whistles. As the advance party made their way up the mountain, they met the group on their way down, only to find that they had been having a 'whistle blowing competition' organized by the so-called leader 'because it was a good way of keeping up morale'.

International Mountain Distress Signal. If you ever find yourself in the unfortunate position of needing assistance when in the

mountains, the International Mountain Distress Signal is six blasts
of the whistle followed by one minute's silence. This should be
repeated until you are located. If you ever hear this signal the
answer is three rapid blasts of the whistle repeated at intervals of
one minute. If, for some reason, you have no whistle, the same
signal can be given using shouts, flashes of a torch, waves of
handkerchief, etc.

Spare clothing. The amount of spare clothing you carry will
obviously depend upon the time of year, whether you intend to
camp (See section 1.6), and your objective. You will invariably
need to take your windproof and waterproofs (although not
necessarily your overtrousers), and a spare sweater.

One of the simplest ways to ensure you have enough spare
clothing is to ask yourself whether you could survive a night in the
open. At low levels on a balmy summer night, survival should not
prove too much of a problem. However, if you are benighted in
winter in the high mountains, you are going to need all the
insulation you can get, and you may even wish to consider carrying
a sleeping bag. A spare pair of woollen socks and a duvet jacket will
prove useful in these circumstances, as will extra sweaters and a pair
of mittens (See section 3.5).

Survival bag. Every person in the group should carry a survival bag.
It is not sufficient for only the leader to carry one. With the
exception of those situations caused by individual injury, if one
person in the group needs a survival bag, it is more than likely that
everyone will need one unless the situation is resolved quickly. A
survival bag is simply a heavy-gauge polythene sack about three feet
wide and six feet long. Although generally very cheap, it is one of
the most important items of equipment that you will ever buy, and it
could quite literally save your life (See sections 3.2 and 3.5). The
silver 'space blankets' are of limited use in the mountains,
polythene survival bags being far more effective.

Emergency rations. Emergency rations can either be bought as
ready-made packs or you can make them up yourself. Not only is
the latter method considerably cheaper, but you can also put exactly
what you want into the pack. The main requirement is energy, so
the best things to choose are those containing large amounts of

sugar, the more common being boiled sweets, barley sugar, glucose tablets, mint cake, dried fruit, and bars of chocolate. Giant-size Mars Bars (and similar) are particularly popular.

Most people find their emergency rations incredibly tempting whilst on the hill. Unfortunately those items which get nibbled are often forgotten and rarely get replaced, so there is always a danger that in a real emergency you might find you have scoffed the lot. The only way around the problem, apart from a stiff dose of self-discipline, is to put all the rations into a plastic bag, then seal it using a whole roll of adhesive tape. I can assure you from personal experience that this is a very effective deterrent.

First aid kit. It is obviously wise to have some form of first aid kit with you. If you are with an organized group, the leader should have a reasonably substantial one with him but even if he has, it is a good idea for you to carry a kit of your own. This personal first aid kit need not be anything complex, although if you visit the mountains alone (when you are experienced) or with one or two friends, it will obviously need to be fairly substantial (See section 3.7).

OTHER ITEMS

The items described above should be regarded as the minimum essential equipment for mountain walking. However, there are various other items which you might like to consider taking along.

A map case can be a useful addition to your gear, for although waterproof maps are available for some areas, they tend to be few and far between. If you decide to buy one, choose a model which has its opening at the bottom, as this will help prevent penetration of moisture. A good map case will pay for itself over and over again, for it will prevent your map from disintegrating due to the common combination of driving rain and strong winds. However, they do have disadvantages, as anyone who has worn one in really bad weather will tell you. Not only do they flap around annoyingly, but also they twist and turn on their lanyard to such an extent that it is easy to imagine they have a mind of their own and are trying to strangle you. Many people prefer to protect and strengthen their maps either with clear adhesive plastic or, better still, with a waterproofing spray.

A good quality insect repellent will prove invaluable at certain times of year. Indeed, if you happen to visit the Isle of Skye at the wrong time, you will think it is an essential. Although the Skye midges are legendary, mountain midges in general have a justified reputation for being horrendously voracious.

Other items which might prove useful include sunglasses, a spare pair of boot laces (often forgotten) and no matter what the time of year, some form of protection against sunburn and windburn (e.g. glacier cream, lip salve, etc). Some people take small squares of closed cell foam on which to sit, others never venture into the hills without a camera or a pair of binoculars. Assuming you always carry the essentials and remember that weight is one of your greatest enemies, these 'little luxuries' are entirely up to you.

WINTER EQUIPMENT

Mountain walking in winter is a totally different proposition, more closely allied with mountaineering. Weather conditions can be severe (See Part two) leading to an increased risk from mountain hypothermia (See section 3.2), and there is the risk of cold injury (See section 3.4). Mountain days become extremely short – especially in Scotland – leading to a greater possibility of benightment (See section 3.5). The chances of a poorly-equipped party surviving an unexpected night in the Scottish mountains in winter are very slim.

Owing to the severity of the conditions, you should regard a good quality (preferably unbreakable) vacuum flask as an essential piece of winter equipment. Most people fill them with either hot soup or some form of hot sweet drink. Alternatively, you can carry the necessary equipment to make a brew whilst on the hill. This will usually consist of a pressure stove (either petrol or paraffin), some form of cooking pot (usually a dixie or billy can), and the necessary ingredients. Gas stoves tend to be infuriatingly slow because normal disposable cylinders contain butane. Due to its vapourizing temperature, this is impossible to light below $-1°C$, so if you do use a gas stove in winter conditions, you should use cylinders containing propane which vapourizes at a lower temperature, albeit only slightly (See section 1.6).

Cooking equipment is obviously far heavier and more bulky than a flask, but if you are camping you will have it with you anyway. However, even when this is the case, many people prefer the convenience of a flask.

Winter days are very short making a torch another essential piece of equipment. Whilst there are many different types available, the most practical for mountain use are headtorches. These have several advantages over the more conventional types, the most obvious being that they leave your hands free and the light travels with your head illuminating where you look. Particularly good (although expensive) are those zoom headtorches in which the batteries are carried at the back of the head. These also have a useful facility whereby you can carry two spare bulbs inside the lamp bezel.

If you take a torch, you will also need something to power it; alkaline batteries should be the natural choice. Although expensive and up to fifty per cent heavier than standard cells, they do last substantially longer, giving over twelve hours light from a zoom headtorch with a standard bulb. Make sure your battery is in good condition before leaving for the hills, and either keep it upside down in the battery case, disconnected, or separate from the torch until you need to use it. There is nothing more annoying than finding that your torch has been switched on accidentally and the battery is flat. Take care also, not to short-circuit the terminals on alkaline batteries (easier to do on some types than others) as this can lead to leakage of electrolytes with consequent damage to equipment and clothing.

In winter, ground conditions can often be difficult and may well require the use of an ice axe and crampons (See sections 4.2 and 4.6). Generally speaking, if there is snow on the hills you should not venture forth without an ice axe. In addition, visitors to any of our major mountain areas will need to be aware of the problems posed by, and the risks associated with, cornices and avalanches (See sections 4.3 and 4.4).

If there is any snow lying on the ground, there will be a risk from snow blindness (See section 3.6). Contrary to popular belief, this can occur even on a dull day and snow goggles or some other form of protection for the eyes should be considered essential.

GROUP EQUIPMENT

Whichever the season, you will find there are various items of
equipment which can either be shared amongst the group, or which
only one member need carry; for instance, at least one person
should have a reliable watch. Many items will be dependent upon
your route and objectives. If you intend to do any scrambling, you
may well consider it prudent to carry a rope. Indeed, many party
leaders consider a rope to be an essential item of equipment when
walking in rocky or rugged terrain (See section 4.7).

When you camp in the mountains, away from habitation, there
will obviously be a number of other items which you will need, and
many of these can be shared between the group (See section 1.6).

In the final analysis, only you can decide what to take and what to
leave behind. Even though I frequently lead groups into the hills, I
never take flares because I do not believe their usefulness justifies
their inclusion. One of my friends, however, considers flares to be
essential items of safety equipment and will not venture into the
hills without them. Who can say which one of us is right?

RUCKSACKS

Even if you only walk in summer, taking the barest minimum of
spare clothing and equipment with you, you are going to need
something in which to carry your kit. For all practical purposes
there is really no alternative to a rucksack. As with clothing and
footwear, rucksacks come in a bewildering array of shapes and
sizes, some of which are totally unsuitable for the mountains.

There is no single ideal size, the capacity needed being dependent
upon a number of different factors. If you intend to camp, you will
obviously need a larger rucksack than if you are simply going for a
short walk. You must also consider that you will invariably need to
carry more kit in winter than in summer, and that rock-climbing or
other equipment can take up a surprising amount of space.

The capacity of rucksacks is usually quoted in litres. As a general
guide, a daysack used purely for hill walking will hold between
twenty and thirty litres, whereas if you intend to do any technical
rock climbing or to carry any specialist equipment you will probably
need a sack with a capacity of between thirty and forty litres. For

winter hill walking, around fifty litres of space will often be necessary, and for backpacking and expedition work, capacities of between sixty and seventy-five litres are common. Generally speaking, if you need more than seventy-five litres' capacity for mountain activities you are either carrying too much or you are not very good at packing.

Many modern rucksacks have compression straps at the sides which enable you to vary their capacity to a certain extent. This is an extremely useful feature as it allows you to use one rucksack for a variety of purposes. Beware, however, of using one which is too large for your chosen activity, for rather than carrying it half full, most people find there is an almost irresistable temptation to fill it, and you will soon find that you are struggling along with a load composed mainly of unnecessary items.

Even with the relatively light weights carried during day walks in summer, the design of the rucksack is very important. In general terms, the more simple and straightforward it is, the better. The basic shape should be such that it allows you to carry the load high on your back, so that the weight acts vertically down your spine. The shoulder straps should be fairly wide and well padded and should obviously be strongly attached to the main structure.

Try to avoid those rucksacks which have a proliferation of pockets and extraneous straps – the less gear you have on the outside, the less cumbersome will be your load. This is particularly important if you intend to go scrambling or climbing. However, if you intend to use the sack in winter you will obviously need facilities for carrying one or more ice axes and a pair of crampons.

Although few daysacks have load-bearing hip belts, some form of waist strap will be found useful for steadying the load during scrambling. Also useful are facilities for adding two side pockets, a large zipped pocket in the top flap, and a haul loop. Most people find canvas backs far more comfortable than nylon, and if there is some form of padded ribbing to increase the amount of ventilation, so much the better.

Rucksacks are made from a variety of different materials ranging from simple nylon, through canvas and cordura, to modern lightweight synthetic fabrics. Although I do not doubt that many of these fabrics are totally waterproof, I have yet to come across a rucksack which can keep all its contents dry in a mountain storm. There are so many seams under stress, so many points where water can find its way in, that the truly waterproof rucksack simply does not exist. For this reason, many committed hill walkers consider polythene bags to be essential items of equipment. Black plastic dustbin liners are extremely useful in this respect and, although less substantial, are far cheaper than purpose made rucksack liners.

Details of rucksacks suitable for backpacking and mountain camping, together with a discussion on the pros and cons of packing your sack, can be found in section 1.6.

FOOD

Whether you visit the mountains to climb, to walk, or simply to gaze at the scenery, you will soon find that you use a considerable amount of energy. It is therefore important that you eat well. Although it is possible to get your energy from the body's stored reserves, it is not good practice and you should aim to get a balanced diet which provides you with a minimum of 4000 kilocalories per day when you are actively walking.

The most important meal of the day is breakfast and because fat is the food which contains the most energy, a good old-fashioned fry-up is ideal. Breakfast should be a leisurely affair because fat takes a long time to digest.

During the day carbohydrates are far better. Although, weight for weight, they contain fewer calories than fat, their energy is available to the body far more quickly. Sugars are more effective than starches, so snacks should be high in sugar. In winter in particular (or on cold wet days in summer) your daytime diet should contain a high percentage of carbohydrate and protein. In extremely hot conditions, you should maintain the level of carbohydrate but reduce the amount of protein. You may also need to increase the intake of salt (See section 3.3).

It is important to have a good evening meal in order to boost energy reserves particularly if you intend to visit the mountains on the following day. This is especially important if you are camping (See section 1.6).

WATER

People commonly underestimate the amount of liquid needed whilst in the mountains, forgetting that water is needed in the reaction which converts food into energy. In fact, dehydration is a far more common hazard than most people realize (see section 3.3). During summer and, surprisingly, in extremely dry cold conditions, the water requirements of the average person can be in the order of one litre per 1000 kilocalories of energy used, which means that you should aim to drink at least four litres of fluid per day. Considerably more than this may be required if you are doing particularly heavy work. Although it is possible to let the body get into a water debt and replace the loss at the end of the day, this can lead to all sorts of complications. For this reason many people regard a water flask as an essential piece of equipment.

Contrary to popular belief, it is generally perfectly safe to drink from high mountain streams. Even if there is a dead sheep above you, its effect on the water will disappear within a remarkably short distance. It is impossible to give definite figures because they depend upon such things as the composition of the stream bed and the speed of flow of the water.

LITTLE AND OFTEN

The generally accepted rule with regard to eating and drinking whilst on the hill is 'little and often'. Although many people like to sit down and have a definite lunch break, it is far better to spread the meal throughout the day. The same applies to drink, particularly to cold drinks which, if taken in too large a quantity, can overcool the stomach and cause stomach cramp.

Many experienced hillwalkers will no doubt be appalled that I have neglected to mention some piece of equipment which they consider to be indispensable. As with clothing and footwear, much of the equipment taken into the mountains is a matter of personal preference. So long as you have the essentials, the rest is entirely up to you.

1.6 **Mountain camping**

Most of the discussion in the previous section assumed that you would be returning to a valley base each evening. Whilst this is the usual programme for most people, you will almost inevitably want to try camping in wild country at some juncture.

Mountain camping has its own devotees and its own unique attractions. Like other forms of mountain activities it can, at worst, be uncomfortable, frustrating, gruelling, and even dangerous. At best, when the routine works and everything miraculously falls into place, it is like no other experience on earth. To sit and watch the sun sink into the horizon, knowing that you and your companions are alone on the mountain, can be a magical experience; to ride out a storm in the same situation can be extremely humbling. Whatever the conditions, there is a certain something, a primitive reality, which seems to increase the further away one gets from habitation. I imagine people feel the same thing when camping in the desert or the jungle or the icy wastes of the Antarctic.

If you intend to camp, you will obviously need a few extra items of equipment including a tent, sleeping bag, stove and dixies, and a larger rucksack. You will also need extra clothing and suitable food, and will soon find that it is often the little things which make camp life comfortable. Some form of routine is essential, especially in wet weather.

Whilst a detailed discussion of camping in wild country is beyond the scope of this book, equipment failure (or omission) can precipitate a number of hazards. A brief description of the essential features is therefore justified.

MOUNTAIN TENTS

Some friends and I once went on an extended backpacking trip through the north-west Highlands of Scotland. The weather was unbelievably good and we spent several nights high up in the mountains, sleeping beneath the stars without there being any need for tents. Whilst the experience was unforgettable and is one which I would thoroughly recommend (given the right conditions), this was very much an exception, and under normal circumstances you will need a good quality tent which has been designed specifically

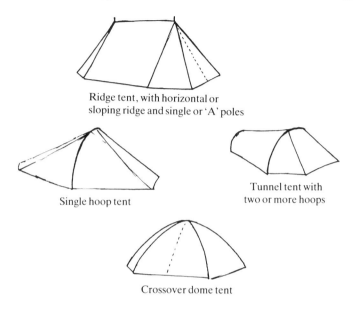

Ridge tent, with horizontal or
sloping ridge and single or 'A' poles

Single hoop tent

Tunnel tent with
two or more hoops

Crossover dome tent

Fig. 3. Basic mountain tent designs

for use in the mountains.

Mountain tents, like everything else, come in a bewildering array
of shapes and sizes (Fig. 3). There are geodesic-dome tents,
crossover-dome tents, tunnel tents, single-hoop tents, horizontal-
ridge tents, sloping-ridge tents, and a variety of strange, hybrid
designs which purport to combine all the best features of their
parents. Some are made entirely from synthetic materials, whilst
others have synthetic flysheets and cotton inner tents. All are
expensive. There are also mountain tents designed for use at high
altitudes in extreme cold/dry climates, and these are totally
unsuitable for the wet and windy conditions which usually prevail in
the British hills.

No matter what the shape, there are certain features which a mountain tent should have if it is to be of any use. It should be light and compact, and relatively quick and easy to erect. Some modern designs seem mind-bogglingly complex until you get to know them, and you should therefore practise pitching your tent before you take it into the mountains. You will find this is particularly important in inclement conditions because, despite what the sales blurb may tell you, the tent which is easy to pitch in a high wind has yet to be designed.

If your tent is to be at all weatherproof, the inner tent should be totally enclosed by the fly sheet, and should have a sewn-in groundsheet, the material of which extends up the walls for a short distance. There should be enough space to allow you to store wet equipment (preferably beneath the flysheet but not in the inner tent), and the design should be such that you can safely cook in, or very close to, the entrance during bad weather.

Most important of all, a mountain tent must be sufficiently stable and robust to stand up to the full gamut of mountain weather. A tent which rains water onto its occupants during a downpour is more of a liability than a help, and a pole which breaks during a storm can literally become a matter of life and death. Do not forget that one missing pole section or a forgotten connection piece can render your tent virtually useless (See section 1.3).

SITES

It is not enough simply to buy a good quality mountain tent; you must also choose a good site on which to pitch it. The main requirement is a reasonable amount of shelter from the wind, but it is unwise to pitch your tent below a cliff – falling rocks can do a lot of damage. You will also find life a lot easier and more comfortable if you choose flat ground free from boulders or tussocks.

Although it is useful to site your camp near some form of water supply, this can lead to problems. The first time I camped in the mountains, I pitched my tent on a flat area of springy grass by the side of a pretty little mountain stream whose musical burblings lulled me sleep. During the night it rained, the burblings quickly grew into a deafening roar, and before I knew what was happening, I was lying in six inches of water. Luckily it was only a heavy shower and the weather was mild, otherwise the situation could have been extremely serious.

PITCHING THE TENT

Once you have chosen your site, pitch your tent with the worst in mind. Face the door away from the prevailing wind, and make sure that the guys are in line with the tent seams and that all the pegs are secure. In soft ground you can put stones over the pegs to give added security, but make sure that there is no risk of the guy chafing. If the ground is so hard that you have difficulty in placing pegs, you may well find it easier to tie the guys around rocks.

In snowy conditions, pegs that are initially loose will often freeze into place, especially if you compact the snow before placing them. If the snow is too soft for this to happen, the easiest way to secure the guys is to tie them around stones and bury them (assuming, that is, you can find any stones). If there is any spindrift (See sections 2.2, 2.4 and 2.7), it will be helpful to compact snow against the base of the flysheet in an attempt to stop the gap between the fly and the inner tent from becoming clogged. If practicable, do not allow snow to build up against the walls or ridge – it is surprisingly heavy and has been known to cause tents to collapse.

On a calm summer evening after a hard day on the hill, all these precautions may seem tiresome and unnecessary. However, as will be seen in Part two, mountain weather can change at an alarming rate, and a fine and settled evening can rapidly deteriorate into a mountain storm. Until you have experienced such weather, it is difficult to imagine how savage it can be, and you will find it far easier to pitch your tent well initially, than get up in the middle of a dark and stormy night in order to alter guylines or secure a flapping flysheet.

SLEEPING BAGS

If a good mountain tent is important, so is a quality sleeping bag. Those filled with down are superb, for they give a large amount of

Wild-country camping in Snowdonia. Camping in such conditions can be exhilarating; it can also be extremely uncomfortable.

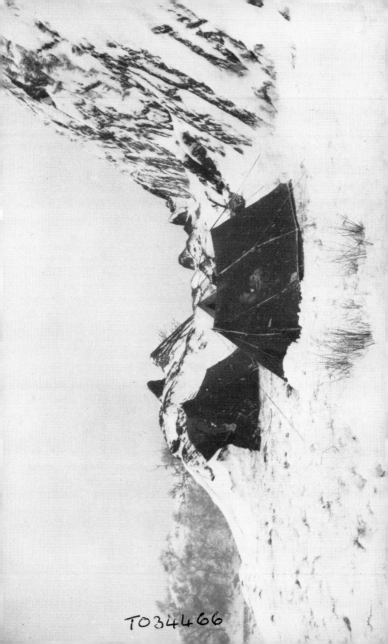

TO34466

warmth for a small amount of weight and bulk. However, not only are they expensive, but they also suffer from the same disadvantage as down-filled duvet jackets in that they lose all their insulating properties if they get wet. For this reason it is essential to keep them dry.

Many people prefer to carry slightly heavier and bulkier sleeping bags filled with synthetic fibres, for these retain much of their insulation even when soaked. Several types of synthetic fillings are available and the more modern are only slightly heavier and bulkier than down. If space is at a premium, it will help to use a compression sack – a stuff sack with straps which allows you to pack the sleeping bag extremely tightly.

The warmth of sleeping bags is rated in seasons, the ratings, somewhat confusingly, going from two to five. A two season bag is suitable for summer use, a three season bag for autumn and spring (and, depending on the quality, possibly valley camping in winter), a four season bag for general winter use, and a five season bag for high level winter camping. When buying a sleeping bag, you should find out the lowest temperature for which it was designed, because different manufacturers have different ideas about average temperatures during the various seasons.

When discussing clothing I stated that thickness equals warmth, and this applies to sleeping bags as well. Most are quilted in order to stop the filling from moving around; if this was not done, all the insulation could end up at one end of the bag leaving the other end full of cold spots. However, if the quilting is done in such a way that the stitches go from the inside fabric to the outside shell, there will be no appreciable thickness of insulation along the line of the stitches, and such seams will themselves become cold spots. There are several ways around this problem; from sleeping bags with two separate layers, each of which is quilted in a different place, to having several compartments separated by box walls (Fig. 4). Additionally, any zip will cause a cold spot unless there is some form of baffle across the opening.

The shape and size of your sleeping bag is mainly a matter of personal choice. As long as it is reasonably light and compact, comfortable, and keeps you warm when you are on the hill, its

Sewn through – cold spots along seams

Slant wall – the most commonly used construction with loose fillings

Sandwich construction – used with synthetic fillings, sometimes with an extra layer between the two sewn through quilts

Overlapping tubes – the most efficient design with loose fillings such as down. Baffles along the length of the tube stop migration from end to end

Shingle – the most efficient design with synthetic fillings, using separate layers or 'batts' of material fixed between inner and outer layers

Fig. 4. Sleeping Bag Construction

shape is about as important as its colour. But remember, if you buy a bag which is too big, you will have to warm a larger volume of air which has a greater chance of being lost from around the shoulders.

What you will also notice, no matter what the season rating or size of the bag, is that cold seems to seep up from the ground. This is because your weight compresses the filling and thus makes it less efficient. The simple way around this problem is to buy yourself a closed-cell foam sleep-mat.

A selection of modern camping stoves and dixies. *From left to right*: Paraffin pressure stove, lightweight gas stove with resealable cartridge, gas stove with non-resealable cartridge, petrol pressure stove, spirits stove complete with pans, aluminium cook-set.

STOVES

If a tent and sleeping bag are important, a stove is essential. After all, if the worse comes to the worst you can invariably find shelter and you should get warmth from your spare clothing. Cooking on a fire fuelled by damp grass can, however, be awkward. Here again, there is the problem of choice, for there are gas stoves, pressure stoves, spirit stoves, solid-fuel stoves, and stoves which profess to burn a multitude of fuels. As you will no doubt have realized by now, there is no such thing as the perfect piece of equipment and each of these stoves has advantages and disadvantages.

So far as serious mountain camping is concerned you can forget the solid-fuel stoves. Although fine as a standby, they are not efficient enough to be your main source of heat.

Gas stoves are undoubtedly the cleanest and most convenient types available, although they are fairly expensive to run, and the spare cylinders (which are bulky to carry) may not be available in remote areas. There are other disadvantages – they turn to burn at an infuriatingly slow rate once the cylinder begins to empty, and, whilst it is tempting to use them to warm up the tent on a cold night, normal butane gas is impossible to light below −1°C. This problem can be overcome to a certain extent by using propane cylinders (if they are available for your type of stove), but on the whole gas stoves do not like cold weather. They are also very sensitive to draughts.

Pressure stoves are probably the most commonly used forms of cooking appliance in mountain camping, even though they are initially fairly expensive. There are a variety of types available, some burn petrol, some paraffin, and one or two claim to burn almost any liquid fuel. Generally speaking they are extremely efficient and economical although, like gas stoves, they tend to work better when sheltered from draughts. Lighting procedures vary from model to model, and it is therefore extremely important that you become familiar with your stove *before* going into the mountains. Many require priming and if this is done incorrectly it can lead to a flare – potentially disastrous if inclement conditions have forced you to cook in the entrance to your tent.

Methylated spirit stoves can also be efficient and cheap to run, and unlike others, they seem to work best in draughty conditions. Although they require no priming (and are therefore very convenient), few models offer the same range of burning rates as pressure stoves. Some of the better spirit stoves come as a complete, fairly compact package, with dixies and other cooking utensils included in the price. If this is taken into consideration, they become an attractive proposition for first-time buyers.

FUEL CONTAINERS

Leaking fuel is a potential hazard with all stoves, especially those using liquids. Methylated spirit, petrol, paraffin, etc are best carried in aluminium containers specifically designed for the purpose. The better of these have deep screw tops with replaceable rubber washers. Safety pouring caps are also available.

COOKING UTENSILS

If your stove does not have built-in utensils, you will obviously need something in which to cook your food. Aluminium cooksets are the most popular as they are fairly light and reasonably priced. The alternative is a set of nesting dixies or billies. You will also need crockery and cutlery, many people taking a mug and one deep plate to act as soup bowl, dinner plate and dessert dish. Although plastic crockery is popular, plastic cutlery tends to be too easily broken to be practical.

COOKING HAZARDS

The most common camping injuries are burns and scalds, and you must be especially careful when using your stove. Wherever possible, cook well away from the tent, and always hold the pot when stirring the contents or adjusting the heat. Make sure that the stove is on a firm base, and concentrate on what you are doing. If the weather is so inclement that it drives you inside, cook as near to the entrance of the tent as possible. Ideally there should be no-one else in the tent with you, but if there is, make sure they keep still. Avoid placing hot dixies directly onto the groundsheet unless you want neat round holes.

Fire and heat are not the only potential hazards. All forms of combustion produce poisonous gases, and if you must cook in the tent, you should ensure that there is adequate ventilation. Changing gas cylinders is also potentially risky, as is leaving your gas stove inside the tent at night. Butane and propane are both heavier than air; any gas escaping from a leaking stove or cylinder will form a layer across the floor of the tent. The sewn-in groundsheet will prevent the gas escaping, and the layer will continue to grow until it reaches nose level, with possibly fatal results.

The backpacking rucksack. Note the way the pack is shaped to fit the contours of the back. Note also the position of the hip belt – around the top of the hips, NOT around the waist.

BACKPACKING RUCKSACKS

When thinking about equipment you should never lose sight of the fact that you are going to have to carry it into the hills on your back. Your load should never exceed one third of your body weight, and with modern equipment should only rarely exceed fifteen kilograms. Whatever the final weight, there is a certain art in packing a rucksack and carrying a load over rough terrain; the better your rucksack and the more efficient your packing, the easier the task will seem.

Choosing a good backpacking rucksack is akin to buying a pair of boots: apart from any other considerations, it has to fit. Like your daysack (See section 1.5) it should be simple and straightforward, designed in such a way that you can carry the load high on your back. It will most likely have a capacity of between sixty and seventy-five litres, and will ideally have an adjustable back and a well padded, load-bearing hip belt which fastens comfortably across the upper part of your hips (*not* around your waist). When the hip belt is adjusted correctly, the weight should bear directly onto your legs through your pelvic girdle. In this way, very little weight is taken by the shoulders, the shoulder straps being used mainly to keep the rucksack in balance.

Other useful features include two (and only two) zipped side pouches, a large zipped pouch (and perhaps, a pocket) in the top flap, and a small side pocket for keys, money, etc. Many backpacking rucksacks have a zipped bottom compartment, and on some models, the baffle which separates this from the main compartment can be unzipped.

PACKING THE RUCKSACK

The aim when packing is to achieve a well-balanced load in which the heavier items are towards the top. You should also consider the order in which you are going to need things. On a day which promises rain, it is not very helpful to pack your waterproofs so that you have to empty everything in order to reach them.

Most people pack their sleeping bag and spare clothing towards the bottom (wrapped securely in plastic bags), and their tent and cooking equipment towards the top. Items needed during the day usually go in one of the pouches and emergency rations and survival bag go right at the bottom. It is perhaps safest to keep your stove and fuel separate from everything else, especially food.

For reasons which become painfully obvious as you walk along, you should try to avoid packing objects with sharp corners and hard edges near the outside of the sack, especially at the back. Many people unroll their sleep-mat and use it to cushion the inside of the main compartment, this having the added advantage that it acts as a waterproof liner. Others use sit-mats or survival bags in the same way

CAMP CUISINE

Carrying all this equipment in addition to walking or climbing is going to use up a fair amount of energy, all of which will need to be replaced. Taking the correct food is therefore extremely important, as has already been mentioned in section 1.5.

The best type of food will be light to carry, reasonably compact, and quick and easy to cook. It should also be fairly appetizing. Despite their reputation, some modern dehydrated foods are very good, especially those which have been prepared by freeze-drying. Unfortunately, these tend to be fairly expensive. The amount of energy (calorific value), size of portion, cooking times and general taste all vary considerably, and if buying a brand you have not tried before, I advise you to check such things carefully. I once spent well over an hour preparing a pre-packed ready-to-cook meal, only to end up with a miserly portion, the taste, texture and goodness of which I can only liken to three mouthfulls of stewed tennis ball. It is, of course, possible that this may have been the result of my cooking prowess. However, beware, there are undoubtedly some diabolical concoctions available.

There are various things which can make your meals a little more interesting. Instant mash, powdered milk and stock cubes are useful and many gourmet backpackers never visit the hills without a tin of curry powder. Other common goodies include tubes of condensed milk and individual portions of jam or honey. Do not forget the salt and pepper. All of these can be removed from their original packing and carried in plastic bags or containers; glass containers are heavy, dangerous, and totally unnecessary.

Logistically, you should plan to have two hot meals a day with numerous nibbles in between (See section 1.5). Bacon is a real luxury for breakfast, and the fat can be used to make fried bread. Alternatively, scrambled egg is very good, and although it can be made from egg powder, many people take real eggs, carrying them in rigid egg-boxes. Do not forget the delights of porridge.

Your evening meal should be substantial and it is important that you cook something hot, no matter how tired you are, nor how difficult the conditions. Stews and curries tend to be the most popular dishes (and the easiest), with perhaps, soup to start. If you can manage some form of dessert (tinned fruit being the obvious example), so much the better. Do not try anything too complicated on your early expeditions – the cordon bleu can wait until your camp routine has settled down.

All your meals should be washed down with plenty of hot sweet drinks such as tea or coffee; the risk of becoming dehydrated is far greater than most people realize (See section 1.5). During the day you should sip 'little and often'. A brew as soon as you arrive at your chosen camp site is not only a great refresher, but also a superb morale booster, especially in bad weather.

Many people trying mountain camping for the first time take far too much equipment, most of which is of little use. Murphy's Law states that on your first trip the weather will be abysmal. Unfortunately, a lack of suitable equipment and camp routine, coupled with bad weather and a gnawing tiredness, inevitably combine to give such an unpleasant experience that the first time automatically becomes the last. This is a great pity and, if it has happened to you, I would encourage you to try again. It will only take one good trip to convert you into a life-long enthusiast.

1.7 Mountain accident procedures

Mountain activities are becoming so popular that, cynical though it may sound, if you visit the hills with any sort of regularity you are almost certain to become either directly or indirectly involved in some form of mountain accident. One of the great traditions of mountain activities is that 'mountaineers look after their own' and you should always be willing to help in a rescue if you are asked.

Whilst a detailed description of mountain rescue techniques is way beyond the scope of this book, and evacuation of unconscious or seriously injured casualties is best left to the local mountain rescue team, *every* hillwalker and climber should know the procedures to be followed in the event of an accident.

It is of little use going to the aid of a fallen climber if you fall off

Mountain rescue practice in winter conditions.

yourself. Nor is it a good idea to treat a suspected victim of mountain hypothermia whilst the rest of the party hang around in the wet, the wind and the cold, thus increasing the likelihood that they too, will become hypothermic. No matter what the accident, nor how serious, the first consideration must be to prevent any further injury, either to the casualty or to others. If the casualty has fallen and is lying on an exposed ledge above a further drop, it may be prudent to secure him (See section 4.7). If conditions are bad, you should also ensure that the rest of the party are sheltered from the worst of the weather. Whatever the situation, the worst thing you can do is rush.

Once you are satisfied that there is no further risk to anyone in the vicinity, you should administer first aid, (See section 3.7). If the casualty is unconscious, you should immediately check that he is breathing and has a pulse, and then take any necessary action. Severe bleeding must be treated with the utmost urgency. Unconscious casualties should be put in the coma position (See section 3.7). If the casualty is conscious, your task will be that much easier because he will be able to tell you where it hurts. Your main job is one of reassurance, easing mental anguish as well as physical pain. The importance of reassurance to the victim of any accident cannot be over-emphasized – it is as essential as physical treatment.

Whatever the situation, however severe or otherwise the injuries, you should assume that the casualty will be suffering from medical shock. Do not underestimate this condition – it can, and does, kill. In order to minimize the effects of shock and to prevent the casualty from becoming hypothermic, you should do everything you can to make him comfortable and keep him warm. This will not only involve giving him spare clothing (dressing him if necessary), but also insulating him from the ground with a rucksack or sleep-mat, or further items of clothing borrowed from other members of the group. It will also be of immense help to get him inside a survival bag, or even to move him to some form of shelter.

Do not move the casualty if there is any possibility of spinal injury. If his injuries are such that he cannot be moved to shelter, it may be feasible to construct some form of windbreak or shelter around him.

If you have the necessary equipment with you, it is a good idea to start a brew. Hot sweet drinks can be crucial to the survival of those suffering from mountain hypothermia or shock, as well as being a good morale booster. However, you should not give liquids to casualties with injuries to the abdomen, chest, or head, nor if there is any possibility of rapid evacuation and subsequent admission to hospital. *On no account* should alcohol be given to an injured person (See section 3.2).

EVACUATION
While you are doing all this, you should be weighing up the situation in the back of your mind, for you will eventually have to decide whether you can evacuate the casualty yourself, or whether you will need assistance. Generally speaking, you should summon assistance in all accidents other than those where (a) the casualty is reasonably mobile (i.e. can walk with help), (b) the injuries are superficial, or (c) the journey down is exceptionally short.

If the casualty can walk with help, get someone else to take his rucksack and make your way off the mountain slowly but steadily, choosing the easiest route (not necessarily the shortest). If the casualty is unable to walk, you will either have to improvise some form of stretcher or find some other means of carrying him. Piggybacks, fireman's lifts, and other forms of lifting by hand are extremely strenuous and generally unsuitable.

A useful aid can be fashioned from a rucksack. Empty the contents (preferably into someone else's rucksack) and loosen the shoulder straps. The casualty then rides in a piggyback position, sitting on the body of the rucksack (with or without extra padding) with his legs through the straps (Fig. 5). This can also be done with a coiled rope, the coils being divided in half and the rope being worn either like a rucksack (Fig. 6) or shared between two people (Fig. 7).

If six or more people are available, you could consider improvising a stretcher. Some books describe the construction of various rope stretchers, of which the best known is the Piggott stretcher (Fig. 8), whilst others go into great detail about rigid contraptions, usually constructed from anoraks and tent poles or something similar (Fig. 9). In my experience, the vast majority of

Fig. 5. Rucksack carry

Fig. 6. One man split rope carry

Fig. 7. Two man split rope carry

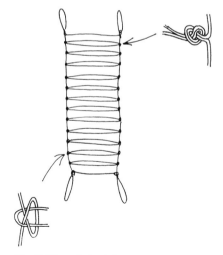

Fig. 8. Piggott stretcher

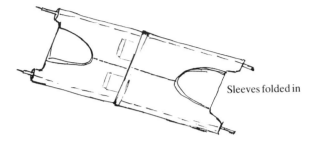

Sleeves folded in

Fig. 9. Anorak & tent pole stretcher

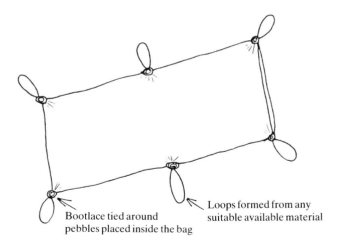

Loops formed from any
suitable available material

Bootlace tied around
pebbles placed inside the bag

Fig. 10. Survival bag stretcher

these dubious structures are about as much use as a chocolate fireguard. Most modern tent poles would pull apart or even break if used for this purpose, and in the vast majority of incidents, it would be far wiser for people to wear their anoraks rather than run the risk of exposure.

At least the Piggott stretcher only uses a rope and whatever padding can be contrived. However, despite what some books tell you, tying one can be a fairly lengthy process (especially on a windy mountainside in gathering dusk) and even when it is constructed properly, it is uncomfortable for the casualty and extremely strenuous for the carriers. If you must build some form of stretcher, it is better to contrive one from a survival bag (Fig. 10) and move the casualty quickly than to hang around trying to get all the knots in the right place.

GETTING HELP

In the most cases where the casualty is too badly injured to help himself, you will need to call for assistance. Help should first be sought from anyone in the immediate area. If no one is visible, use the International Mountain Distress Signal (See section 1.5). Some people use flares, the two star red flare being the accepted signal to request assistance, although any red flare will do. However, to be of any use, the flare must be projected high into the sky, and such types will be fairly hefty, very expensive, and require the purchaser to have a firearm certificate. Even if it does reach a satisfactory altitude, the visibility has to be good and someone has to be looking in the right place at the right time for it to be seen at all. Moreover, by the time its position has been noted, it will have drifted some distance on the wind.

Mini-flares are light and compact, and do not generally require the purchaser to have a firearm certificate. However, they tend to be highly susceptible to wind, and have a reputation for being unreliable particularly in stormy conditions (when you are most likely to need them), often reaching a height of little more than five or six metres before either fizzling out or simply being blown into the ground.

If you happen to hear or see any of these signals (or an SOS), you should immediately take a compass bearing on the signal and then give an answer (See section 1.5). If you are not in a position to investigate safely yourself, you should make a note of your position and the bearing of the signal, together with any other information which you think a rescue team would find useful, and make your way as quickly as is safely possible to the nearest mountain rescue post or telephone (dial 999, ask for the police, then mountain rescue).

MESSENGERS

There is, of course, no guarantee that your distress call will be answered, so it makes sense for a messenger to go for help, provided this can be done safely. If two people can go together, so much the better. It is important that the rescue team has certain information, and this should be written down in order to prevent confusion or mistake. Some people carry a waxed luggage label and chinagraph pencil in their first aid kit specifically for this purpose.

The rescue team will need to know the *exact* location of the casualty. You should therefore give a grid reference correct to at least six figures, preferably eight, together with as detailed a description as possible of the location and the area surrounding it. Include compass bearings on prominent known points. If the accident has happened on a rock climb, you should give the name of the crag, the name of the climb, and the number of the pitch. The team should be able to go straight to the casualty using this information alone.

You should also write down the time the accident occurred, the number of people injured, and the nature of the injuries. Brief details of the number and experience of other members in the party will also be useful.

This information should be taken either to a mountain rescue post or to a telephone, whichever is the easier and quicker. Do not forget that the shortest route is not necessarily the quickest. If you arrive at a mountain rescue post, someone there will know exactly what to do; if you arrive at a telephone, you should dial 999 and ask for the police, and then for mountain rescue. You will be asked a number of questions, some of which may seem to have little bearing on the incident. These questions are asked for a reason, and you should answer clearly and concisely. You will usually be told to wait by the telephone either for further instructions or until someone arrives. Do not worry if you have no money on you – these emergency calls are free.

PROTECTING THE CASUALTY

If you are left with the casualty, make sure he is as comfortable as possible, and keep reassuring him. Watch his vital signs and do any necessary first aid (See section 3.7). Make sure that the rest of the group remain in shelter, and – assuming you have the necessary equipment – make plenty of hot sweet drinks.

In general, you should never leave an accident victim by himself. However, if two of you go into the mountains together and one of you has an accident, you may find you have to leave the casualty in order to fetch help. This will not be an easy decision to make. Before you leave, you should make sure the casualty is sheltered and as comfortable as possible and give him all your spare clothing. He will very likely be suffering from shock, and it could be many hours before help reaches him, during which time the weather conditions could easily worsen. Unless you take the utmost care before you leave, he could easily die.

It is extremely important you mark the position of the casualty as prominently as possible. He should be in a survival bag (usually bright orange), but if you can mark the area with other bright objects, so much the better. Cairns of stones can be useful, as can a climbing rope stretched out across an otherwise featureless slope.

If the casualty is unconscious, consider what would happen if he regained consciousness and moved. If he is on a ledge, you may well have to secure him in some way (See section 4.7). Leave a reassuring and cheerful note in a prominent position so he does not feel totally abandoned if he regains consciousness and finds himself alone.

If the casualty is conscious, reassure him, make sure he is as comfortable as possible and leave him a whistle and a torch. He can use these to keep signalling which may help guide the rescue team to him.

Whatever the situation, any messengers have a grave responsibility, for a life may depend upon their speed. However, it is better to arrive late than never and, as they are bound to be tense, they should take greater care than usual as they descend towards the nearest telephone or mountain rescue post.

Part two

Weather conditions

2.1 Introduction

No matter where in the world they are situated, mountains are almost always colder, wetter, and windier than lowlands. Whilst weather plays an important part in the formation of the mountain scenery and certainly has much to do with the often awe-inspiring sense of majesty which can be found in such surroundings, it is also both directly and indirectly responsible for a number of hazards.

One of the major difficulties with which you will have to contend is simply coping with the weather. If you could guarantee that a sunny day would stay sunny, or even that a rainy day would stay rainy, it would be relatively easy to dress and plan accordingly. However, there is an incredible variety of weather to be found in the mountains, and it is this variety which causes the problems, particularly as conditions can swing from one extreme to another with frightening speed, often within the space of a few hours.

Mountains make their own weather. They force moist air to rise, and form a barrier to the wind, often causing it to funnel through narrow gaps. For this reason, as the Meteorological Office will be the first to admit, no weather forecast can yet be relied upon to give details of all the local peculiarities of a mountain area. General forecasts will therefore have to be interpreted with caution, and you may well have to modify them in order to get an idea of the type of weather that can be expected in the mountains.

Wherever you are in Britain, you are never far from the coastline. This proximity to the sea causes British mountain weather to be far less predictable than that found in most other parts of the world. Even after years of experience, weatherwise locals may get it wrong. Indeed, it is possible for walkers in one valley to be struggling in wind and rain, whilst in the next valley, their companions are climbing on a sun-drenched crag.

Once you realize the incredible variety of conditions, their rapid changeability, and – in the British mountains at least – their unpredictable nature, you can perhaps understand how it is that so many people underestimate mountain weather, particularly in winter. Not only does proximity to the sea make the weather difficult to predict, but it also causes the conditions to be far more severe than would otherwise be expected. It is a demonstrable fact that weather conditions in the British mountains can be as severe as those met in the Alps, *if not more so*.

Generally speaking, the higher you go, the more likely you are to meet severe weather. You should therefore take extra care when visiting the higher and more northerly peaks in Scotland. Here, the weather can be so unexpected as to be bizarre. I was once caught in a monumental blizzard on Suilven in mid-August. On the other hand, I have also spent a beautiful day in shirt-sleeves on An Teallach in February.

No matter what the season, it is only prudent to assume that the worst conditions may occur, and go suitably equipped (See sections 1.4 and 1.5). However, as we have discussed, weight is your enemy, and you should certainly not go to the ludicrous extreme of taking full winter kit in summer, purely on the off-chance that the weather might turn particularly nasty. You may laugh, but I've seen it done.

In this part of the book we will look at the various weather conditions you can expect to meet in the British mountains, and discuss the ways in which they may affect you, both directly and indirectly. To take a simple example; the direct effect of rain might be to make you wet, but it could also effect your progress indirectly by causing poor visibility and by wetting the rocks, thereby making them slippery.

The final section in this part of the book is concerned with basic weather forecasting, for an appreciation of weather and how it is caused is an integral part of mountaincraft. This does not mean you have to get bogged down in technical details; to be weatherwise, all you need is a little understanding and a lot of observation. As with all the other components of mountaincraft, skilled weather

The Cefn Cwm-llwch ridge disappearing into a sea of cloud. Even when the valleys are dismal, the tops can be clear of fog.

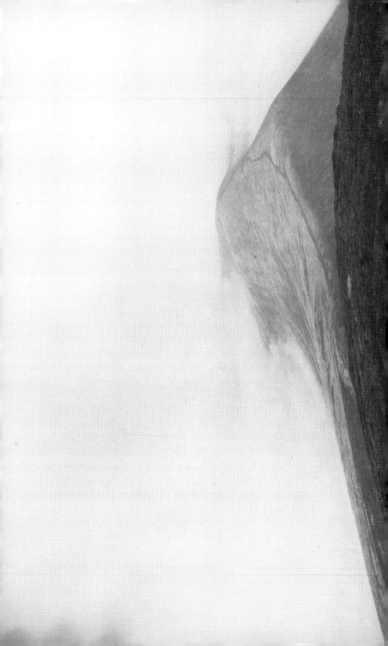

forecasting only comes with experience, and that cannot be taught in a book. For this reason you should never dismiss the advice of local climbers, friendly hill farmers, etc, for they will know better than you what the local mountains do to the national weather.

Although you should not be afraid of the weather, you should be prepared to change your plans and even retreat if the weather turns nasty. Striking a happy balance between the two is often extremely difficult and it is always better to err on the side of caution. However, those people who only visit the mountains on clear, calm, sunny days and retreat at the first sign of cloud will undoubtedly miss some memorable experiences.

2.2 **Poor visibility**

Whether we like it or not, poor visibility is a fact of life in mountain areas. Some people stay away from the hills in such conditions because they feel their enjoyment will be lessened by the lack of extensive views; others keep to the valleys because they are concerned about getting lost. Whilst there is nothing wrong with either of these points of view, they often cause people to miss what would otherwise be an enjoyable day. There is more to visiting the mountains than simply gazing at the view, and good navigation will prevent you getting lost.

Two particular experiences will, I hope, serve to illustrate my point. The first occurred in North Wales when there was thick cloud down over the tops. Although the two people with me were initially apprehensive about the lack of visibility, we spent a memorable day scrambling on Tryfan and Glyder Fach. Far from being lessened, our enjoyment was enhanced by the poor visibility – the atmosphere of the ridges with their rocks disappearing into the mist all around us was overwhelming. Despite not seeing a single panorama, it was a day which stayed in my mind.

The second example occurred in the Brecon Beacons, on a day

Cloud over the summit of Pen-y-Fan. Cloudbase is not always stable. A few minutes after this photograph was taken, the summit was clear of cloud, but by the time we had reached it, it was covered once again.

when the valleys were heavy with fog. Having trudged up the
northern slopes and on to the ridge below Corn Du in abysmal
visibility, we suddenly emerged from the fog just past the Tommy
Jones memorial. Immediately it felt warmer: we had walked
through a temperature inversion (See section 2.3) and above us was
a deep-blue sky. The visibility was superb. The temperature
inversion lasted all day, and when we finally and reluctantly
dropped back into the ocean of fog and returned to the valley,
no-one but experienced walkers could understand why we were
waxing lyrical. The thing to remember is that just because it is dull
and gloomy first thing in the morning, it does not necessarily mean
that it is going to remain that way all day, nor that it is dull and
gloomy everywhere else.

CLOUD
The most common cause of poor visibility is cloud, minute droplets
of water which slowly sink through the air. This is not really
surprising when you consider that many of the clouds which occur
over Britain have bases below 1000 metres, whilst many of the
mountains are higher than this. Indeed, stratus cloud (See section
2.10) can have its base below 300 metres and, if it is raining, the
cloud may be thousands of metres thick.

Mountains can also make their own clouds by forcing air to rise.
If this air is moist enough, some of the water vapour it contains will
condense into droplets as it rises and cools. On the other side of the
mountain, the air may descend, in which case it will warm up and
the cloud will disappear (See section 2.8). Cloud which hugs the
mountains is often known as hill fog.

In certain circumstances, ridges can trap thin layers of cloud
causing one side of a mountain to have poor visibility whilst the
other side is clear. It is also possible for clouds to form in a valley in
the early morning and sit there until the sun reaches them and burns
them away. These clouds are more often known as fog. Both these

Lyn Llydaw from the summit of Snowdon. Note the cloud rushing in on the left.
Conditions can change remarkably quickly. Within seconds of taking this photograph
the visibility was less than twenty metres.

conditions are associated with temperature inversions (See section 2.3).

Do not forget that the cloudbase is not stable. Although generally speaking it only rises or falls slowly, it can move remarkably quickly if there is a squall or if it starts to rain. Do not get caught unawares.

If the cloud is down over the tops, you should be aware that it may cause indirect hazards. Cloud is formed from water droplets, therefore it will make both rocks and people wet. Wet rocks can be slippery; wet people can easily become very cold unless properly clothed (See section 1.4). In addition, if the ambient temperature drops below freezing point, clouds can form rime, a feathery white ice which coats rocks (See section 2.3). Although pretty to look at, this can make progress difficult.

If, like me, you are bearded it is an uncomfortable experience when the water droplets freeze in your beard. You may look like a rugged arctic explorer, but the sensation of meltwater dribbling down your neck is not a pleasant one. The ice which forms is also impossible to remove by any means other than melting – a hazard if you call in for a warm and a pint on your way home, for you tend to drip in an embarrassing fashion.

OTHER FACTORS
Although cloud is the most common cause of poor visibility (all types of ground-level cloud are often referred to as mist), there are several other factors which you should consider. Heavy rain, for example, can be almost as restricting, and strong winds blowing directly at you can bring tears to the eyes making it extremely difficult to see. If a headwind is carrying either rain or, even worse, hail, it can be virtually impossible to make any progress, simply because it is too painful to look where you are going (See sections 2.5 and 2.6).

If rain and hail can be a problem, snow can be even worse. When combined with strong winds, even gently falling snow may become a

Walking in mist. Note full waterproofs. Route finding across rough terrain (such as that shown in the picture) in poor visibility requires good navigation techniques.

blizzard, a severe condition in which it can be impossible to make any progress (See section 2.7). Even if there is no snow falling, the wind can whisk up snow lying on the ground forming spindrift. This can swirl in waist-high layers (making it difficult to see your footing) or in layers several metres thick (making it difficult to see anything).

Even in relatively calm winds, when snow falls through cloud and there is already snow on the ground, you can be faced with a white out. In this condition you will find it impossible to judge distances and horizons, and will probably spend much of your time falling over. Your companions will appear to float, and you could literally be standing on the edge of a precipice without realizing it. The only way to tell whether the ground rises or falls is to throw something in front of you. In such conditions, pin-point navigation and extreme caution are essential.

No matter what the cause of the poor visibility, it can be potentially hazardous in a number of ways. You will find the thicker the mist, the easier it is to lose all sense of time, and this can lead to the danger of benightment (See section 3.5).

COPING WITH POOR VISIBILITY

There are various ways of avoiding potential problems. Good navigation is obviously of paramount importance, especially if you are not following a well-defined path. In such conditions you will not only need to know how to interpret your map, but also how to follow compass bearings and estimate times and distances with a high degree of accuracy. This is particularly important when you are in featureless terrain, or when there is a covering of deep snow.

Even if you are following a well-defined path, you must take care and concentrate on the job in hand. Use all the identifiable features you can to pinpoint your position whenever possible, and take extra care when you are nearing junctions. Experience will soon show you that it is very easy to walk straight past what is normally an obvious junction. At best, this will cause confusion and delay, at worst, it may cause benightment (See section 3.5).

Although often known as hill walkers' friends, you should be wary of cairns. Usually they point the way and are extremely useful. However, some popular paths and peaks are becoming so heavily cairned that you could quite happily walk around in circles for hours.

If you do suddenly find yourself lost, *don't panic*. The two worst things you can do are (a) rush off blindly in the hope that you will find something which will guide you back on course, and (b) push on regardless because you refuse to admit that you don't know where you are. What you should do is stop, sit down, and think about it. Ask yourself what could have gone wrong, then do something to correct the mistake. If you are on a path, *do not leave it*, it is a definite feature which must lead somewhere. If you are not on a path but in the middle of nowhere, try to find some form of definite feature which you can identify both on the map and on the ground. More detailed discussion of navigation in poor visibility and relocation techniques will be found in my book, *Mountain navigation techniques*.

Finally, route selection becomes especially important when you cannot see where you are going. Truncated spurs and convex slopes are extremely hazardous as descent routes; the further you drop, the steeper they get. This means you cannot see what is coming even in good visibility, and may find yourself on dangerously steep ground before you realize what has happened. Although you should try to select routes which are easy to follow, it is generally not a good idea to follow streams. Water takes the line of least resistance and will quite happily flow over the top of a cliff.

2.3 Temperature

There can be summer days when it is so hot that you will long to find some form of shelter but find it difficult to summon the energy to move. There will also be days in winter when it is so cold that it hurts the back of your throat to breathe, and the icy wind brings tears to your eyes. Both these extremes of temperature present potential hazards to the mountain visitor.

Judging by the clothing worn by casual walkers following the more popular paths (e.g. the Llanberis path up Snowdon or the Storey Arms path up Pen y Fan), some people think that if the temperature in the valley is 15°C, the temperature on top of the mountain will be 15°C. This is seldom the case. Generally speaking, the higher you climb, the colder it will become. The rate of change of temperature with altitude is known as the lapse rate (See section 2.8), and this can be so great that it is possible for the summit of a mountain to be below freezing point when the valley is relatively warm. The height at which the temperature reaches 0°C is known as the freezing level.

In certain circumstances the valleys can be colder than the tops. When this happens, meteorologists will tell you that there is temperature inversion. Although the causes do not really concern us, it is important that you know they can exist, learn how to recognize them (or at least when to expect them), and understand the ways in which they will affect conditions.

Ground inversions usually occur on calm nights when dense cold air flows down from the mountains. In its mildest form, this can give rise to pockets of cold air known as frost hollows (Fig. 11), in which the temperature may be as much as 5°C lower than that of the mountain slopes. A more serious form is when the cold air becomes trapped in the valley, and lies in a sheet across the valley floor, the coldest air sinking to the bottom (Fig. 12). This layer can be several hundred metres thick and can make judging the temperature of the tops extremely difficult. It can also make camping in the bottom of the valley an excruciatingly cold experience, and campsites on the lower slopes of the mountain are often warmer.

Ground inversions often cause heavy dews and thick fog. They can be seen in graphic detail in spring and autumn when white frost coats the valley sides up to a certain height and then stops. Both fog and inversion usually disappear shortly after the sun's warmth reaches them. However, if the valley is so deep that it rarely gets any sun, the inversion can last for days.

An inversion can sometimes form half way up the mountain, in which case it is known as an inversion aloft (Fig. 13). This can be extremely difficult to detect, and can cause sudden changes of temperature if it rises or sinks. Your only clue may be a thin layer of

Ice shining on the East Moelwyns. In such conditions an ice axe should be considered an essential item of equipment.

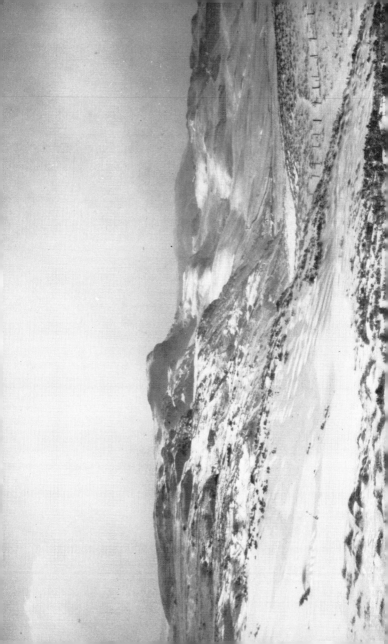

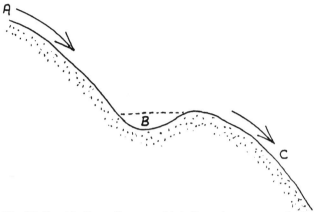

Fig. 11. Frost hollows. Dense, cold air flows down mountain slope
A and collects at **B** to form a Frost Hollow. Further cold air
continues **C** towards the valley floor

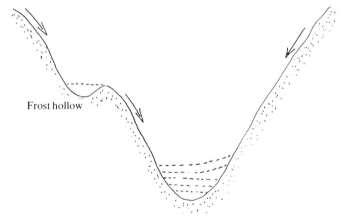

Fig. 12. Temperature inversion. Dense cold air has reached the
valley floor, and because it is a calm night, it remains there, the
colder air sinking to the bottom (cf. Fig. 11)

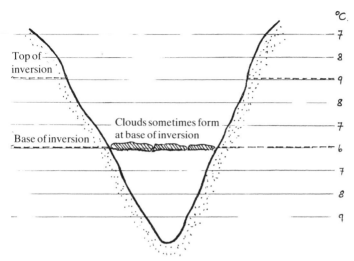

°C

Top of
inversion

Clouds sometimes form
at base of inversion

Base of inversion

Fig. 13. Inversion aloft

cloud half way up the mountain.

It is not only the ambient temperature which causes us to feel hot
or cold; other factors include clothing, exercise, rain, and wind.
Light winds often make the difference between comfort and
discomfort on a hot day, but if combined with rain, they are icy cold
and can lead to windchill (See sections 2.4 and 3.2).

COLD TEMPERATURES
Whatever their cause, cold temperatures bring with them a number
of potential hazards, the most important of which concerns the
body's response. If you feel cold when you are in a centrally-heated
house, you turn up the boiler; if you feel cold on the mountains,
your body will turn up its heating mechanisms. This leads to a
greatly increased consumption of energy, and if this goes
unchecked, and the heat loss is not corrected, the inevitable result
will be exhaustion-exposure, more correctly known as mountain
hypothermia (See section 3.2).

If you go into the mountains in extremely cold conditions with insufficient protection for the hands or feet, the body will automatically reduce the blood flow to the extremities in an attempt to stop the heat loss. This process is known as *vaso-constriction*, and is one of the factors affecting the occurrence of frost-bite (See section 3.4). If, on the other hand, you have gone prepared and are wearing a number of pairs of gloves and socks, this in itself may restrict the circulation and have the same effect. It is for this reason that the clothing and footwear you use (at any time of year) should not restrict the circulation in any way.

Even when there is no chance of frost-bite or frost-nip, the temperature can still be low enough to cause potential hazards. When the wind blows and the rain falls, your hands can become numb with cold. Normally this is more of a nuisance than a hazard, causing frayed tempers (because it takes half an hour to untie your bootlaces) or sober embarrassment (because you drop the jar of beer for which you have been craving all through the descent). However, numb hands can be hazardous (particularly when rock climbing or scrambling) causing you to fumble with ropes and knots, and lose your sense of grip on the smaller handholds. Moreover, if you feel cold, you will tend to huddle into your clothing and miss much of what is going on around you. The simple way to avoid these problems is to wear sufficient clothing (See section 1.4).

Cold temperatures can affect the ground conditions as well as the body, often causing hazards which have a beauty of their own: heavy deposits of rime, which commonly form when cloud droplets freeze on objects exposed to the wind, may build up into large flakes totally covering the object in a surreal layer of dull white feathers; hoarfrost, which occurs when water vapour crystallizes as ice on solid objects, causes each fragile crystal to twinkle and shimmer with a life of its own. Sometimes the vapour crystallizes on snow, forming a glittering layer of surface hoar.

One of the more common cold-weather hazards is verglas, a very clear, wafer-thin layer of ice which can make rocks treacherous. Although this usually exists only in freeze-thaw conditions, when it is formed by a thin film of meltwater freezing on rock surfaces, it can arise directly, when super-cooled raindrops freeze on contact with cold rock.

Even simple water ice causes a fair number of problems, especially when it coats the well-worn and easy paths of summer. Although we usually bunch snow and ice together, they can exist separately, and frequently do so. Freezing rain can form thick sheets of ice, even when it falls on grass, and there is little doubt that this type of surface can be lethal to a careless party when slopes overlooking a steep drop are affected. It is best to avoid all such surfaces unless you are equipped with crampons and know how to use them (See sections 4.2 and 4.6).

HOT TEMPERATURES

If cold can cause hazards, so too can heat. Heat exhaustion and heat stroke are potential killers (See section 3.3), and dehydration is far more of a hazard than is commonly realized. Apart from these and the other ailments mentioned in section 3.6, heat can sap your strength leaving you feeling dizzy and lethargic. In the same way that you need to protect yourself from heat loss in cold weather, you may have to protect yourself from heat gain in hot weather. This is one of the few occasions in the mountains when it can be good to sweat, for the evaporation of body moisture can be an effective way of losing heat.

In really hot weather, make sure you wear a sunhat of some description, and do not underestimate the value of a good sunscreen. Avoid strenuous exercise during the hottest time of day, and drink plenty of liquid (See section 3.3).

CHANGES OF TEMPERATURE

Whilst the two extremes of temperature have their own potential hazards, changes from one to the other can also cause problems. A thaw will melt snow, thereby increasing the amount of water in streams (See section 4.8), and generally making conditions underfoot difficult (See section 4.2). It will also weaken cornices (See section 4.3) and may cause avalanches (See section 4.4).

Often overlooked is the chapter of stonefall due to the freeze-thaw action (See section 4.5). I am particularly wary of this, having been pelted with fist-sized rocks on numerous occasions whilst walking below the limestone cliffs near my home. The process is very simple. During cold spells, the moisture in cracks and crevices freezes, expanding as it does so and thereby cracking the rocks. The ice so formed holds any loose rock in place until a thaw, when the rock either falls, or the gap behind it fills with water. This water later freezes, and so the process begins again, each successive frost loosening the rock more and more. Be careful when walking below large cliffs in such conditions.

Finally, sudden changes of temperature from hot to cold can also be extremely hazardous. As an example, I quote a tragic accident which occurred in Snowdonia. On a warm spring day, early in the season, a young hill walker reached a peaceful mountain lake and, finding the water too inviting to resist, stripped off and dived in. What he did not realize was that the water, having so recently been snow, was only a few degrees above freezing, whilst he, having just finished a steep climb, was extremely hot and sticky. The shock of entering the icy water was so great that it killed him.

2.4 **Wind**

Whether a light breeze or a fierce gale, wind will be your constant companion whilst you are on the hill. Total calms are so rare as to be almost non-existent and even when they do occur, they seldom last for any length of time. On hot days in summer, a gentle cooling breeze will be most welcome, and you will think of the wind as your friend. Generally speaking, however, wind creates more problems than it solves.

It is impossible to appreciate the ferocity of a wall of air until one has hit you. I was once with a party which climbed from Ogwen Cottage to Bwlch Tryfan on a day when the wind was gusting strongly from the north-east. As we reached the col, we lost the shelter of the mountain and were exposed to the full force of the

The north face of Corn Du. Note that aspect of slope can affect the conditions. North-facing slopes retain a sprinkling of snow and ice far longer than their southern counterparts.

wind which was being funnelled through the gap between Tryfan and the Bristly Ridge. One fairly well-built member of the party was proudly wearing a new, voluminous, cagoule-style jacket which covered not only his body but his rucksack as well. He was in the process of telling us (for the umpteenth time) what a good idea it was when, on reaching the head of the valley, a particularly fierce gust got underneath this strong, nylon garment, inflated it so he looked like the Michelin man, and bodily lifted him over the remains of a dry stone wall, dumping him unceremoniously on the other side. I will never forget the look of pained surprise on his face as he flew by, his feet level with my elbows. Luckily only his pride was hurt, but I never saw him wearing that cagoule again.

EFFECTS OF LANDSCAPE

The behaviour of air flow in relation to topography is an extremely complex subject, and a full discussion is well beyond the scope of this book. Although you should know that wind speed usually increases with height, the amount of increase and the relationship between wind speed and altitude alters from area to area and day to day. Due to ground friction, air moves faster at height even over a plain, but when it reaches the mountains, a number of other factors come into play.

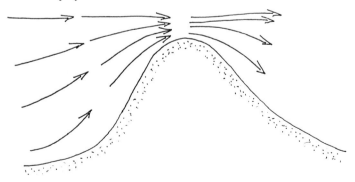

Fig. 14. Weir effect. Winds usually speed up when blowing over mountains

In order to understand the way in which topography can affect the wind, it will be helpful to imagine that air cannot rise above a certain level (this, in fact, is not far from the truth), and to compare the movement of air with the movement of water. When wind reaches the mountains, the same amount of air has to pass through a small space, it therefore increases speed in much the same way as water going over a weir (Fig. 14). Similarly, wind increases its speed when forced through a valley in the same way as water flowing through a sluice gate (Fig. 15). If for some reason the air cannot rise above a mountain, it may flow around it like water flowing around an island, causing the wind speed to increase across the shoulders of the peak (Fig. 16). Unstable air usually climbs over a mountain,

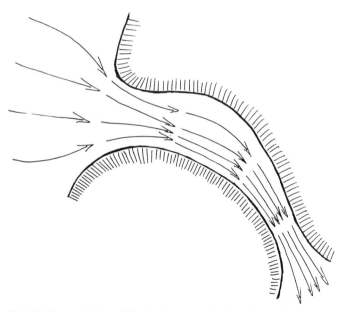

Fig. 15. Venturi effect. Winds often speed up (and sometimes change direction) when forced through narrow valleys

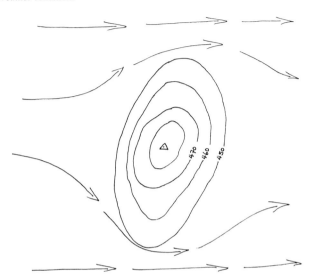

Fig. 16. Island effect. Wind sometimes speeds up over the shoulders of an isolated peak

whereas stable air is more likely to seek a way around it (See section 2.8).

By likening air flow to water flow, you should be able to predict local increases in wind speed, and even some local changes in direction. But, be warned, it does not always work.

TURBULENCE
One important effect which, somewhat confusingly, can be both helpful and a potential hazard, is turbulence. This may be caused in several ways. Leeside eddies form when the wind blows across a sharp ridge or any sudden change in the angle of slope (Fig. 17). The main wind continues to rise at the top of the steepest slope, and it can cause an eddy in which a weaker wind will blow in the opposite direction. It is this process which is largely responsible for

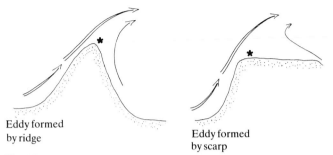

Eddy formed by ridge

Eddy formed by scarp

Fig. 17. Leeside eddies. ★ indicates approximate position of null point

the formation of cornices (See section 4.3).

Where leeside eddies are formed at the top of a ridge, there is often a null point, just below the top and on the lee side, where the winds are extremely light. Null points can be used to great advantage if you are being buffeted by a strong wind when ridge walking, for they present a corridor of calm along which you can travel quite easily. However, unless the ridge is remarkably uniform, null points are not as stable as some people seem to think. On sharp or rocky ridges in particular, sudden or unexpected gusts can quite easily overbalance you, with potentially serious consequences. When following null points, watch the ground around you for signs of approaching gusts.

If wind blows across a series of ridges, rising on one side then sinking on the other, it can generate a wave pattern often recognisable by lines of parallel, stationary clouds. If these waves grow to any size, the wind can become extremely turbulent and form a rotor (Fig. 18). If the base of this is near the summit of a mountain or the crest of a ridge, it can cause sudden, strong and totally unexpected gusts in the opposite direction to that of the main wind. This can obviously be very dangerous. Indeed, rotor was the most likely cause of a fatal accident on Pen y Fan, when a person who rather incautiously leant into the wind to look down the north-east face was blown over the edge by a strong gust coming suddenly from behind.

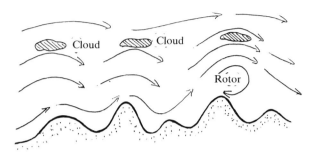

Fig. 18. Rotor. Note increased strength of wind in area of possible rotor and lines of stationary clouds

STRONG WINDS

A surprising amount of energy is required to walk against a strong wind. This is not only because of greater physical effort, but also because any increase in wind speed will act in exactly the same way as a decrease in temperature, especially in wet conditions. This effect is known as windchill, and will be discussed in detail in section 3.2.

The sheer power of the wind is illustrated by the incident of the airborne cagoule. Even if the wind is not powerful enough to make progress difficult, a headwind will slow you down, and remember, the friendly following wind which helped you to the summit will become a hindering headwind when you turn to go home. If the wind is blowing harder than Force 6 (Fig. 19), you will soon start to feel that you are fighting an invisible enemy. Apart from the extra physical effort needed, such a battle can be incredibly frustrating.

The situation is even worse when the wind is gusting, for extra energy is needed to keep in balance and to push against the sudden increases of pressure. If the wind gusts harder than Force 8, you will find yourself being blown over; if it blows a steady Force 9, you will probably be unable to make any progress except by crawling. Being

Strong winds can be a serious problem, and may even blow you over.

Force	Forecast Name	Speed kph	General Details
0	Calm	<1	Lakes calm as a mirror; smoke rises straight up; no effect on fresh snow.
1	Light	2–5	Wind just felt on face; smoke drifts slightly; no effect on fresh snow.
2	Light	5–10	Vegetation trembles; ripples on lake; no effect on fresh snow.
3	Light	10–20	Heather moves; wavelets on lake; some surface drifting of fresh snow.
4	Moderate	20–30	Small branches move; dry grass blown about; spindrift up to one metre.
5	Fresh	30–40	Small trees sway; difficult to pitch tent; widespread drifting.
6	Strong	40–50	Walking requires extra effort; large branches move; spindrift above head.
7	Strong	50–60	Large trees sway; danger of being blown over; near blizzard conditions.
8	Gale	60–75	Walking near impossible with large rucksack; small branches break; blizzard.
9	Gale	75–90	Crawling difficult; standing impossible; large branches break.
10	Storm	90–105	Body dragged along by wind; trees uprooted.

Fig. 19. The Beaufort Wind Scale

caught in conditions like these can be extremely frightening, for there is nothing you can do to stop the wind. If you cannot claw your way safely off the mountain, you may have to find shelter and sit it out (See section 3.5).

Anyone who has ever tried to fold a map in windy conditions will tell you that it is virtually impossible. More seriously, the stronger the wind, the more difficult it becomes to read your map and to work out bearings. If the wind speed increases above Force 6, sighting on bearings can be difficult, and you may need someone to shelter or steady you whilst you read your compass. It is in conditions like this that you will be glad of a route card (See section 1.3).

Whilst the wind speed can increase dramatically in squalls, visibility can decrease just as suddenly. Any form of precipitation carried by the wind is going to reduce visibility, but it can be blinding if the wind is in your face. Hail is undoubtedly the most painful (See section 2.6), but rain can be almost as bad (See section 2.5). Snow tends to blow everywhere, and airborne powder snow or spindrift can make you feel as if you are suffocating (see section 2.7). A freezing wind in winter can bring tears to the eyes, as can a hot, dust-laden wind in summer. Snow-goggles or sun-glasses may help.

Finally, and more specifically for rock climbers, wind can be a major hazard on exposed rock faces, especially when gusts threaten to pluck you from your holds. Even if the climb is sheltered, the noise of the nearby wind can make communications difficult or even impossible, and unless you know your rope partner well, you may well find that you have to rely on tugs on the rope. This, in itself, can be potentially hazardous, especially if flurries of wind occasionally confuse you by plucking at the rope.

2.5 **Rain**
Mountains affect rainfall in many different ways, most of which are fairly complicated. Whilst you need not know the complexities, it will be useful to have an appreciation of the basic principles.

In the simplest terms, mountains make their own rain. They form a barrier to the wind, and so can force air to rise (See section 2.4), causing it to cool and lose some of its moisture (See section 2.8). This moisture can condense either as cloud or as rain, depending upon the concentration. Any such rain is known as orographic rain, and is in addition to the cyclonic rain associated with frontal systems (See section 2.10). Furthermore, mountain barriers can physically slow down fronts, causing cyclonic rain to last for far longer than would otherwise be the case. It is not surprising, therefore, that mountains are far wetter than lowlands.

Not only is rain more common in mountain areas, it also tends to be heavier. This, again, is due to a number of fairly complex processes, some of which are concerned with the condensation of atmospheric moisture from turbulent air. We have already seen that the frequency of rain is increased because both orographic and cyclonic rainfall occur; when the two occur at the same time, or when turbulence causes mist droplets to join together to form rain, the intensity of the rain is increased.

Unfortunately, it is difficult to quantify these processes because hardly any figures are available. The most valuable data come from the records of the Ben Nevis Observatory which operated from 1883 to 1904, and which show that the Ben was far colder, far more cloudy, and far wetter than nearby Fort William. Looking specifically at precipitation, more modern figures estimate the annual rainfall on the summit of Snowdon to be twice that of Capel Curig (12 kilometres away and 900 metres lower), and six times that of the Cheshire Plain.

Rainfall tends to be heavier on the windward slopes than on the lee slopes. Rising to pass over the mountain barrier, the air will shed some of its moisture and therefore be drier when it reaches the other side (Fig. 20). Having passed over the barrier, the air will begin to sink and warm up, and will be able to carry more water vapour. This is known as the Föhn effect (See section 2.8), the drier area on the leeward side of a mountain range being known as the rain shadow.

A large proportion of the rain which falls over Britain and Europe starts life as snow at altitudes of above 10,000 metres. As it descends into warmer air, it begins to melt, first forming sleet (partially melted snow) and then rain (See sections 2.7 and 2.8). Each raindrop may take hours to fall, during which time it is at the

The River Usk at Crickhowell after heavy rain. Fed by mountain streams (which rise and fall far more quickly than large rivers), rivers such as the Usk can give awesome illustrations of the power of water.

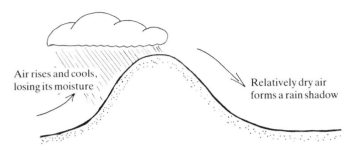

Fig. 20. Rain shadow

mercy of the wind and may travel a considerable distance. This tends to negate the rain shadow effect to some extent, and is one of the reasons why Capel Curig, nestling below the mountains of central Snowdonia and sheltered from the prevailing winds, has approximately three times as much rainfall as the Cheshire Plain.

COPING WITH RAIN
You should be prepared for rain whenever you venture into the hills, even if the forecast is good. Occasional light showers in the valley usually indicate frequent heavy showers in the mountains, and lowland drizzle can quite easily become a highland downpour. Surprising as it may seem, August is one of the wettest months, with October, November and December contributing to the wettest quarter. Conversely, May and June are usually the driest months.

Different types of rain bring different types of problems. Squally showers bring increased wind speeds and decreased visibility, and many people consider them to be worse than steady rain because it is difficult to know whether to stop and put on waterproofs or to carry on regardless. They seem to have an annoying habit of stopping as soon as you have put on your waterproofs, then starting again as soon as you have taken them off and packed them away.

The situation is not as fraught as it used to be – breathable fabrics have made life far less uncomfortable. When I first started visiting the mountains, those of us who could not afford ventile would avoid wearing our proofed-nylon cagoules for as long as possible, knowing that we would become just as wet from condensation as we would from drizzle. However, wearing a cagoule at least makes sure that the moisture warms up and stays put, and this can be extremely important because it is not the dampness which is hazardous, but the evaporation (See sections 1.4 and 3.2). One of my friends used to be in the habit of putting on his cagoule only in torrential rain, arguing that so long as he kept walking (and therefore kept producing heat) he would come to no harm. One moist day he underestimated the effects of windchill and was carried off the mountain suffering from mountain hypothermia (See section 3.2). Had he worn his cagoule, it is more than likely he would have completed the walk without any ill effects. There is a lesson here for us all.

No matter how good your clothing and equipment, walking in steady rain can be depressing. With your shoulders hunched, your head down and your hood well up and closed, your world becomes a small patch of ground which splatters mud and moisture as you trudge along. Lost in your own thoughts, your vision restricted by your hood and the weather, it is all too easy to let apathy and lethargy take over. This can be particularly hazardous if you are camping in the mountains, and is one of the reasons that some form of camp routine is so important (See section 1.6).

CAMPING IN RAIN
If you find yourself camping in wet weather, it is essential that you change into dry clothes and cook yourself a hot meal every evening. You should ensure that you always have one set of dry clothing for use in camp. If you are unable to dry your wet clothes overnight, you may be faced with the horrendously uncomfortable prospect of having to put on wet clothes in the morning, but it is far better for you to do this, than wear your dry clothes and run the risk of getting them wet.

CLIMBING IN RAIN
Climbing and scrambling in the rain brings its own problems. Even if the rock is good and the water does not affect the friction, the

process of reaching for handholds can send gallons of freezing water streaming down your sleeves.

In heavy rain, routes which follow gullies or grooves can become impassable. A friend of mine insists that he was almost drowned during an unexpectedly fierce downpour which caught him half way up the Great Gully of Craig yr Ysfa in the Carneddau.

Exceptionally heavy rain can cause minor landslips on steep mountain slopes, and may cause rockfall in gullies (See section 4.5). River crossings will also be more hazardous than usual (See section 4.8).

RAIN IN WINTER

In winter, when the freezing level is low, it is possible that rain which falls steadily over a long period of time can cool the air around it sufficiently for the moisture to turn to sleet or even to snow (See sections 2.7 and 2.8). This can occur even when there is no mention of snow in the weather forecast. If cloud is down over the mountain tops, it may be concealing fresh snowfall even when it is only raining in the valleys.

If it rains on a day when the temperature is hovering around freezing point, look out for verglas and icy patches on rocks and paths.

As unpleasant as rain can be, it can also lead to some spectacular effects. The only time I have seen a triple rainbow, each one bright and complete, was in the Torridon region of Scotland. Rain also keeps down atmospheric dust. This is why the visibility is so sharp and clear after a shower.

2.6 Hail

My first experience of a mountain hailstorm was above Codale Tarn in the English Lake District. As we reached the top of Sourmilk Gill and walked past Easedale Tarn, we could see large cotton-wool clouds towering over the Langdale Pikes. In total ignorance of the possible significance of these clouds, we made our way up the side of Blea Rigg. Suddenly, what appeared to be a wall of cloud rolled towards us with incredible speed. Before we knew what had hit us, we were in a veritable maelstrom of gusting turbulence and shooting ice pellets which stung our faces and made it impossible to move. We crouched on the ground, shocked into painful submission.

It stopped as suddenly as it had begun, the swirling mass of wind, cloud and ice rushing across Grasmere Common towards the Wythburn Fells, leaving us gasping in its wake. The sun shone warm in a deep-blue sky, but the ground around us was white with hailstones, the grass flattened by the violence of the wind.

Hail is almost always associated with cumulonimbus clouds and often falls during thunderstorm (See section 2.9). The stones themselves are formed when water droplets are caught in the turbulence of a rapidly ascending air current. As they rise, they freeze and continue to grow as more water vapour freezes on their surface. Eventually they become too large to be supported by the air current, and so they fall, often still growing on the descent.

Although the vast majority of hailstones are spherical with a diameter of slightly over five millimetres, they can be of almost any shape and size. Indeed, there are authenticated reports of hailstones weighing in excess of two pounds, and some can have edges which are sharp enough to cut when driven by a strong wind.

Walking into a hailstorm can be an extremely painful exercise and you will undoubtedly be unable to see where you are going. If you are ever caught in a severe hailstorm, you will probably find it best to sit it out (but see also section 2.9). It is highly unlikely that such a storm will last for any appreciable length of time.

2.7 Snow

The pretty, white, fluffy stuff which occasionally falls in your back garden bears only a passing resemblance to mountain snow. This is especially true after it has reached the ground. In this section we are concerned mainly with the snow which is falling or has only recently fallen. The remainder of the cycle of snow will be discussed in Part four.

Snow is formed from tiny ice crystals. These delicate and (under the microscope at least) beautiful crystals are formed when

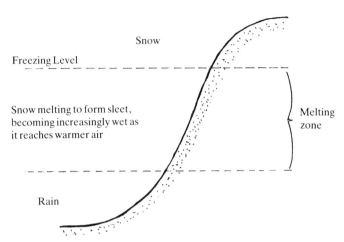

Fig. 21. Melting zone. The melting zone may be over 250 metres
deep

atmospheric water vapour is subjected to sub-zero temperatures
and freezes. Sometimes, particularly when it is very cold, the snow
will fall as individual crystals. On other occasions, when it falls
through a temperature inversion, the snow may partially melt and
then be refrozen resembling soft hailstones. If the air is at, or just
above freezing point, the crystals will be soft and sticky often
joining together to form large clumps.

Snowflakes do not melt immediately on reaching air with a
temperature above freezing point. First the flakes become softened
and wet, possibly forming large clumps as outlined above; then they
will slowly melt. At this stage they become known as sleet. Sleet
continues to fall through air which is now above freezing, melting all
the time and eventually turning into rain. This process may take

The Llanberis Pass. As the snow falls into the valley it starts to melt so that it has
become mostly sleet by the time it reaches the floor.

place over a vertical distance of more than 250 metres, starting from the freezing level (Fig. 21). This means that if the freezing level is at 1500 metres, the falling snow may not totally melt until below 1250 metres. Add to this the fact that the freezing level can move up and down quite rapidly under certain conditions, and you will realize that predicting the height of the snowline can be extremely difficult.

If the snow turns to rain, and the rain continues for any length of time, this in itself can cool the air sufficiently to lower the freezing level (See section 2.5). If this happens under the cover of low cloud it can quite easily take parties by surprise, because the lowering of the snowline will not be visible from the valley.

If snow falls in misty conditions when there is already snow on the ground, it may cause a white out (See section 2.2). Although this is rare south of the Scottish Highlands in anything but winter conditions, when it does occur it can be extremely dangerous, for it becomes impossible to tell the difference between the snow that is falling and the snow that has already fallen.

BLIZZARD

When wind and fresh snow occur together, they can cause a serious reduction in visibility. Due to wind speed increasing with height (See section 2.4), what seems like a small snow flurry in the valley could easily be a raging snowstorm on the tops. The problem of spindrift has already been described in section 2.2, but if the wind freshens to any marked extent, even if no new snow is actually falling, you could be faced with blizzard conditions. You can live with spindrift – you could die in a blizzard.

I have only once been caught in a serious blizzard. It was during a climbing club winter meet in Scotland, and it is not an experience I should like to repeat. The sheer fury of the wind; the numbing, paralysing cold; the snow which felt like sand, hurting, rasping and blinding as it ploughed an almost cataclysmic course across the mountainside. Even if there had been shelter within a few hundred metres, I doubt we could have reached it if it had been upwind of

Snow on Llangynidr moors. Note the squall giving reduced visibility just left of centre.

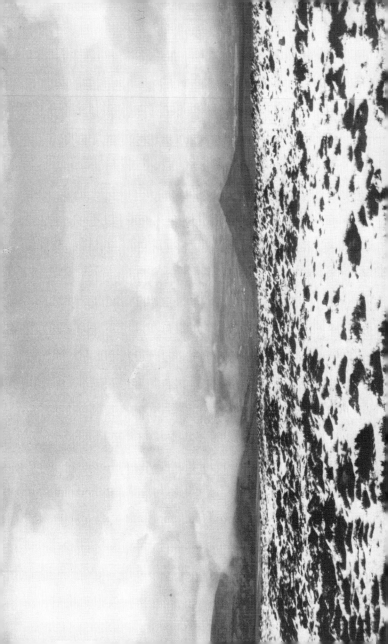

us, for it was almost impossible to breathe when trying to face the weather. Even now, the thought of having to walk into the storm, having to push a way through what, at the time, appeared to be a solid, violent, suffocating wall of snow and air, is one which sends a shiver down my spine. We did the only thing we could. We turned our backs to the wind and found the quickest way off the mountain in that direction. Had that quickest way been further than it was . . .

There is only one wise way to cope with a blizzard, and that is to retreat before it gets too bad. We were lucky that day, a couple of us knew the area well and we eventually found our way down safely. We should have retreated far earlier than we did instead of letting youthful exuberance run away with us, and transgressing one of the unwritten rules by pushing on regardless. Looking back on the experience, I now know how close we were to death. The lesson has been learnt.

OTHER HAZARDS

It does not need a blizzard for snow to create problems. Even on a calm day, fresh snow can camouflage or even totally cover what are normally well-defined features with surprising speed. If the weather has been particularly cold, verglas and patches of water-ice may lie undetected under a thin covering of snow – a potentially lethal combination near the top of a crag. The climber's life is made difficult as handholds and footholds on scrambles and climbs become choked or hidden. The dull acoustics of snowy weather can cause communication problems, and falling snow can reduce visibility and create route-finding problems for all mountain users.

If there is any wind, these problems increase, for not only does the snow have the amazing ability to get into sealed rucksacks and through zipped tent flaps, but also drifting can cover cairns and fill hollows, hindering progress and making route finding problematic. Windblown snow can form bridges across streams, the fragile crust

Winter conditions in the East Moelwyns. Note the snow covered lake. Smaller pools may well be camouflaged by drifts around their edges.

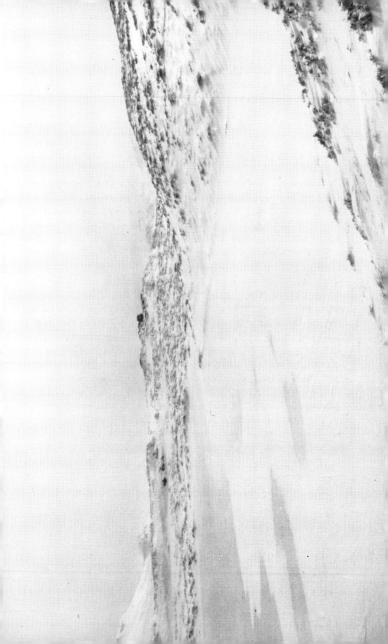

waiting for an unsuspecting ankle. Potentially far more dangerous are drifts covering frozen mountain pools, sometimes camouflaging the banks to such an extent that it is virtually impossible to tell that a pool is there – until you fall through the crust.

Windblown snow can create another hazard – cornices. These are overhangs of snow which occur along the tops of ridges or escarpments and can go undetected if approached from the upwind side (See section 4.3).

If cornices are hazardous, avalanches are worse. The popularity of skiing in the Scottish resorts has at least brought the danger of avalanche to public awareness. Even so, it can still safely be said that avalanches in the British mountains constitute a far greater hazard than most people realize. It is not sufficient to know about falling snow, one must also know what happens to the snow after it has fallen; this will be discussed in section 4.4.

Once the snow has reached the ground, it begins to undergo a number of changes. From being loose and unconsolidated, it slowly changes into a more solid mass which, if at an angle, can effectively hinder progress just as much as if it was a deep drift (See section 4.2).

Few people would deny that a journey into any mountain area in winter is a far more serious proposition than the same journey in summer. However, there is little doubt that it can also be rewarding, for snow-covered mountains have a magic all of their own. The well-trodden paths of summer disappear and the hills seem somehow bigger, more rugged. Adventures are easier to find, and memorable days are there for the picking.

The Llanberis Pass. The effects of altitude show up clearly in this photograph – the snow line is at a similar height on either side of the valley, and at the far end.

2.8 **Effects of altitude**

In the Bernese Oberland region of the European Alps there is an incredible railway. Completed in 1912, it climbs from Grindelwald, nestling in the valley below the Eiger, to the Jungfraujoch, a high mountain pass between the Jungfrau and the Monch, at a height of 3,475 metres. To reach this pass it travels in a tunnel hewn through the Eiger and the Monch for a distance of eight kilometres. It is a justifiably popular tourist attraction, and in the station at Grindelwald there is a large notice written in several languages, warning that people who suffer from any form of cardio-vascular complaint should not make the journey because of the rarified atmosphere of the Jungfraujoch.

The higher one climbs, the greater the reduction in atmospheric pressure, and the less oxygen there is to breathe. Whilst this is obviously a major hazard in such areas as the Himalayas, the Andes, and the Alaska Range, it is generally not regarded as a climbing hazard in the Alps, and certainly not in the relatively tiny mountains of Britain. However, this reduction in atmospheric pressure does have a number of very important effects.

LAPSE RATE

Referring to Fig. 22, let us imagine that the wind consists of parcels of air. When these parcels reach a mountain barrier they are forced to rise, encountering less and less atmospheric pressure as they do so. The air expands because of this reduction in pressure and, as a direct consequence, it cools. This is one of the main reasons why the mountains are colder than the lowlands (See section 2.3). The rate of cooling with increased height is known as the lapse rate.

The cooler the air, the less water vapour it can hold. As most of the air which crosses Britain contains a fair amount of water vapour, there will come a time when the rising parcels of air become saturated. When this happens, it is said to have reached the dew point, and any further cooling, or increase in altitude, will result in the water vapour condensing. When this happens, the water droplets so formed will either create clouds or, if clouds are already present, they may form drizzle or rain. This is one of the main reasons why mountains are cloudier and wetter than the lowlands

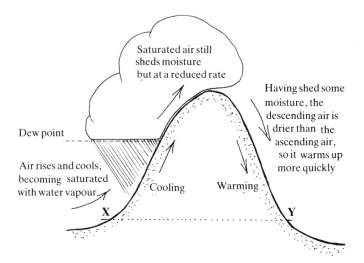

Fig. 22. The effects of altitude. Due to the Föhn Effect, the temperature at **Y** will be higher than the temperature at **X**

(See sections 2.2 and 2.4). Wet air cannot cool as fast as dry air, therefore the lapse rate will become less once the dew point has been reached and the air is saturated.

After it has passed the mountain barrier, the cold saturated air will begin to descend, warming as it does so. Having shed some of its moisture, it will be drier than it was before it met the barrier, and will therefore warm more quickly. This is known as the Föhn effect, and can result in the wind on the leeward side of the mountains being 1°C to 2°C warmer, even in Britain. In the larger mountain ranges the difference in temperature can be substantial and can result in a warm and often turbulent Föhn wind which can trigger wet avalanches (See section 4.4).

The value of the lapse rate is not constant, but varies with the water content of the air; the average in the British mountains is approximately 2°C per 300 metres. However, on windy days or when the air is particularly dry, this may increase to more than 3°C per 300 metres. Conversely, if the air is saturated as it will be in clouds, the lapse rate may drop below 1.5°C per 300 metres. There are very few places in the world where one can find lapse rates greater than these, and this helps to explain why British mountain weather can be so severe. Generally speaking, the arrival of high winds will tend to increase the lapse rate whereas the arrival of low cloud will tend to reduce it.

In winter the air is usually colder. This means that it cannot hold as much water vapour as in summer and may therefore become saturated that much quicker. One result of this is that lapse rates tend, on average, to be lower in winter than in summer. In practical terms, the temperature difference between the valleys and the mountain tops is usually less in winter than in summer.

Lapse rate will affect the way in which the air behaves when it reaches the mountains. If the rate is high, the air is said to be unstable and it will climb fairly easily over the barrier. If, on the other hand, the rate is low, the air is said to be stable and will tend to try and flow around the barrier rather than over it (See section 2.4).

OTHER CONSIDERATIONS

No matter what the lapse rate, the higher you go, the more likely you are to run into inclement weather, simply because conditions become more severe with height. You should also consider the fact that a varying lapse rate can lower the freezing level dramatically whilst you are on the hill. This means that the wet path you followed on your way up the mountain can become icy by the time you return.

Finally, high winds increase the lapse rate as well as the windchill effect. Particularly in winter, this can result in unexpectedly severe conditions on the tops.

2.9 Lightning

Although lightning cannot be regarded as a major mountain hazard, it is responsible for two or three fatalities every year. Without doubt, a major contributing factor is ignorance or misunderstanding; even amongst relatively experienced people who visit places where electrical storms are more common, there appears to be a surprising lack of awareness of any of the potential hazards other than that of a direct hit.

Depending upon whether or not they have ever been caught in a thunderstorm, mountain enthusiasts tend to have one of two attitudes towards lightning. Those with no direct experience tend to be blasé, simply because they do not know what to expect; those who have experienced the awesome power tend to be fatalistic. Both attitudes are wrong, for whilst there is no doubt that lightning can pose a serious threat, that threat can be minimized by the correct action.

There are three main potential hazards which are directly related to the electrical activity in lightning. These are direct strikes, ground currents, and induced currents. As we will see later, there are also a number of peripheral hazards. In order to appreciate both the danger and the ways of avoiding it, it is essential that you understand the mechanisms which operate when lightning strikes.

Thunderstorms are caused by electrical activity in the atmosphere. Electricity, like water, always flows along the line of least resistance, the material through which it flows being known as the conductor. If the electricity flowing through a conductor is powerful enough, it will jump across gaps causing a bright flash or arc, a principle which has been put to practical use in a car's spark plug.

Air is normally a poor conductor, but when subjected to sufficient electrical pressure it ionizes, thus enabling it to pass an electrical current. In very simple terms, during a thunderstorm the clouds become so highly charged with electricity that they ionize the air around them and allow the electricity to arc to earth. This causes the bright flash which we know as lightning.

Following the path of least resistance, the current will invariably take the shortest route through the air, and will therefore tend to strike the most prominent feature in its locality. Over flat land this will be directly below the cloud, but if the ground undulates to any great extent (as it does in the mountains) the shortest distance could

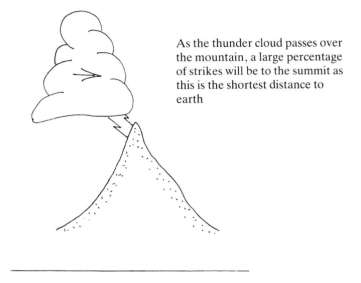

As the thunder cloud passes over the mountain, a large percentage of strikes will be to the summit as this is the shortest distance to earth

As the thunder cloud passes through the valley or reaches the mountain slopes, strikes will be made on upstanding areas of ground, boulders, trees, etc.

Fig. 23. Strike Zone

be to a nearby summit, or even to a boulder or a tree on a mountainside (Fig. 23). However, lightning does not always strike the most prominent features; it often strikes the weathered boundary between two beds (or layers) of rock, because these usually contain moisture and mineral deposits which make them excellent conductors.

The lightning flash is not, in fact, a single spark. Just before the main flash, a small spark known as the leader moves relatively slowly through the air, ionizing it as it goes. This forms a channel of conduction along which the main spark can travel at speeds of up to one hundred times faster.

GROUND CURRENTS

The story does not end when the lightning reaches the ground. Far from simply stopping or disappearing, the electrical current acts in a way which is very similar to that of an egg being dropped onto a concrete floor from a great height. It does not just break – it splatters everywhere. In this case, however, the splattering is not random. As before, the electricity, which is now in the form of ground currents, follows the lines of least resistance and will therefore concentrate its attentions on damp cracks and moist gullies, using up its energy as it goes. On solid rock which, in a thunderstorm will usually be wet, the most likely path is straight across the surface, possibly linking patches of lichen or soil. If there are any gaps in the conductor, the current will often arc across them rather than find a longer way around. The current is losing energy all the time so the further away from the strike, the less its intensity.

INDUCED CURRENTS

Contrary to popular belief, metal items do not actually attract lightning, but they can have electrical currents induced in them when in the immediate vicinity of a strike. These induced currents will, however, be small when compared with the intensity of both the main strike and the subsequent ground currents.

MAJOR HAZARDS

The most obvious hazard to humans is electric shock, either from a direct strike or from ground currents. Although induced currents are usually so small as to be of little danger by themselves, when combined with the effects of ground currents they may make the difference between life and death.

There are two major factors which will determine the amount of injury a person suffers from an electric shock. The first is the amount of current received; the second the part or parts of the body through which this current travels.

A person bridging a conductor (i.e. sheltering from the storm in a damp gully) will present an alternative path for the ground currents. Due to the composition of the human body, it may well be easier for the electricity to flow through the person than along the gully floor. The amount of current which passes through the body will depend upon the distance from the strike, and the position of the person in relation to the conductor. The larger the area of conductor that is bridged, the greater the amount of current that will be diverted.

The worst situation is that in which the current flows through the body in such a way as to affect either the brain, the heart, or the breathing reflex: thus a current which passes from one hand to another is extremely serious because it will pass through the heart and lungs. Most serious is a current which passes from head to foot as in a direct strike, because this will affect almost every organ in the body. Even a weak current following either of these routes can prove fatal, whereas it is possible to survive a far stronger current which passes from one foot to another through the legs.

Even if the electricity is not of sufficient intensity to kill outright, large currents can cause severe and deep burns both at the point of entry and of exit. Mild shocks travelling through the body can cause spasms and semi-consciousness leading to obvious hazards for those people who are struck whilst climbing, scrambling, abseiling, or traversing steep ground. More accidents are caused by falls after having been indirectly struck than by actual electrocution.

Crouching to avoid ground currents. Note that the hands are wrapped around the knees and not placed on the ground. Note also the use of a large boulder.

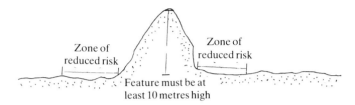

Fig. 24. Zone of reduced risk

AVOIDANCE OF DIRECT STRIKES

From what has been said above, it should be obvious that it is of paramount importance to get away from those areas most likely to receive a direct strike. Peaks and projections should be avoided; there is often an area around them which receives comparatively few strikes. Such features must be at least ten metres high, the low strike area around them being of roughly the same distance horizontally (Fig. 24). Some books have referred to this area as a safe zone, but this is misleading, for it is not one hundred per cent safe. It is impossible to guarantee where the lightning will strike, and there is the added danger from ground currents. Rather than call it a safe zone, it would be more accurate to call it a zone of reduced risk.

If you are caught in more open country, such as on Dartmoor or the Cairngorm plateau, it is advisable to find a place where nearby projections are closer to the clouds than you. The basic rule is to make sure that your head (or any other part of your anatomy, for that matter) does not represent the shortest distance from cloud to earth. For this reason you should try to avoid spurs and the ends of ridges.

If you are in a forest during a thunderstorm, try to find shelter in an area of trees which are shorter than their fellows.

AVOIDANCE OF GROUND CURRENTS

Once you have reduced the risk of a direct strike, you should find a place where you can sit out the storm without being struck by a ground current. The most attractive places for ground currents are damp crevices, cracks, and gullies. These you should avoid. Rather than shelter in depressions, it is better to find a shallow rise or a small, detached boulder.

It will probably be raining, and a natural reaction is to shelter below an overhang or in the entrance to a cave. Unfortunately, this is totally the wrong thing to do, for many such places are simply local widenings of crevices which form the preferred routes for ground currents. If the current arcs across such gaps you may be severely burnt.

If the cave is deep, it may be safe to shelter in it provided there is at least three metres of headroom and one metre of space on either side. However, try to avoid the natural urge to explore too far or you may end up as a cave rescue statistic, rather than a mountain rescue statistic.

AVOIDANCE WHEN CLIMBING

If you have been climing or scrambling and are on a ledge in a dangerous position, you should try to retreat. When this proves impracticable, your best chance is to crouch towards the outside lip of the ledge, if possible leaving at least a metre and a half of space between you and the main rock wall. If you are a long way above the ground and there is any risk that you may fall if stunned, you should tie yourself to the rock (See section 4.7), avoiding using the rope as a jump lead between you and any crevice which might conduct a ground current. In order to reduce this risk, make sure the rope passes around the lower part of your waist. On no account should you tie it under your arms.

ABSEILING

Abseiling (See section 4.7) during a thunderstorm is an extremely dangerous practice, and should be avoided whenever there is a possible alternative. However, if abseiling is the only practicable means of leaving the main strike zone, only go as far as is necessary to escape from the worst of the danger. Two rope lengths is usually more than enough. The rope itself can act as a conductor, so you should try to rig some form of safety rope – if you have a choice, use a dry rope rather than a wet one.

SITTING IT OUT

Once you have chosen a spot which appears to be safe, sit, stand, or crouch taking up as little surface area as possible. If standing, keep your feet together; if sitting, bring your knees up towards your chin, wrapping your arms around your legs. On no account should you put your hands on the ground for this will allow ground currents to pass through your vital organs.

If you can insulate yourself from the ground via a sleep-mat or coiled rope, so much the better. These will obviously be more effective if they are dry, but by this time you will probably have your shoulders hunched against torrential rain, or hail.

Although induced currents are not a major threat, it is wise to take them into consideration if you are anywhere near the main strike zone. At distances of less than thirty metres from a possible strike, you would be well advised to temporarily set aside any metal objects, including pack frames and tent poles. Items stored in your rucksack need not be unpacked and there is no need to abandon any equipment.

PRIOR WARNING

We have been talking about the avoidance of strikes and ground currents as if lightning were something which happened suddenly and without warning. Happily, this is rarely the case. In the vast majority of instances you will be able to see and hear a thunderstorm approaching long before it poses any potential threat. Thunder can be heard up to twenty kilometres away, and lightning can often be seen from distances in excess of a hundred kilometres. As sound travels more slowly than light, it is possible to approximate the distance of a storm. Time the delay between the lightning and the thunder; count in seconds and divide the result by three to get the distance in kilometres. If it appears that the storm is coming your way and you can gauge the windspeed, you can use this figure to estimate how long it will be before the storm will reach you.

Other forms of advance warning tend to be somewhat unsettling, although, in themselves, they present no danger. Due to the ionization of the air, your first warning may be the distinctive tang of ozone. The ionizing may also cause metal objects to hum and spark, and small projections to glow with the eerie, pale blue light of St Elmo's fire. Your hair may hum, crackle and stand on end – it may even feel quite painful, as if someone is pulling your hair. All of this can occur when the nearest clouds are miles away.

EXPLOSIVE DISCHARGES
There is one final hazard which should be taken into consideration, especially in forests or when in the vicinity of steep and rocky ground. We have already seen how electricity takes the path of least resistance, and that this can involve both local projections and damp cracks. When a bolt of lightning strikes, the moisture in its immediate path will be instantly vapourized, and the expansion this causes may lead to explosions. The power of a strike is so great that trees may not simply explode because of the vapourizing of their sap, but may also burst into flames.

The main hazard in the mountains is not so much one of burning trees (although with the amount of forestry around nowadays, you may well be faced with the problem), but that of stonefall (See section 4.5). If the lightning strikes a rock and immediately travels through a damp crack, the water in the crack will be vapourized, expanding to such an extent that it can prise rocks away from the cliff. If the rock is porous and saturated with water, it can literally blow it to pieces. In practical terms this means that, even if you are well away from the strike zone and far enough down the mountain not to be affected by ground currents, it is very unwise to shelter from a thunderstorm below a cliff.

2.10 Basic weather forecasting
The British have a reputation for being a nation of weather haters, possibly with some justification, for no matter what the conditions, we always seem to find something to criticize. Weather conditions play such a large part in mountain activities that you will find they become one of the dominant topics of conversation whilst you are replacing lost moisture in the local hostelry or café.

It is important that you know something of the causes of the various weather conditions, for they affect almost everything you do whilst in the mountains, sometimes helping your progress, occasionally increasing the hazards. By reading previous sections in this part of the book, you should (hopefully) begin to appreciate how mountains modify existing weather. However, in view of the fact that conditions can change so rapidly and radically, it will also be useful to know (a) how that existing weather was caused in the first place, and (b) the various signs which indicate impending changes.

NATIONAL FORECASTS

Modern meteorology is an extremely complex science in which computers and satellites are playing increasingly important roles. It therefore makes sense to use a professional forecast as a foundation upon which to build a picture of the weather you can expect to meet in the mountains. There are a number of different forecasts available from a variety of sources.

Newspaper forecasts, sometimes accompanied by a weather map, vary greatly in quality. Some simply give a report on what the weather has been doing, whereas others stick their necks out and predict what the weather will be doing. When looking at any accompanying weather map it is important to find out whether it is a report map (of past weather) or a forecast map (of possible future weather).

Somewhat better are television and radio forecasts. These have the advantage of being updated between each bulletin. Television forecasts, in particular, are very useful because the satellite pictures give a graphic illustration of the different types of weather. Indeed, some of the forecasters are very good at explaining various features.

LOCAL FORECASTS

National forecasts are useful for getting details of such things as major frontal systems, air streams, etc (see below), but you would be well advised to get a more detailed forecast whenever possible. Recorded forecasts are available by telephone in many parts of the country, details are given in the local telephone directory. Some local radio stations in popular mountain areas broadcast special forecasts.

Forecasts for specific areas can often be obtained from local meteorological forecast offices (also in the local telephone directory). In the major mountain areas it is usually possible to get a general synopsis, together with details such as mountain and valley weather, temperature inversions, lapse rate, freezing level, cloud level and amount, precipitation, wind speed and direction at various heights, temperatures at various heights, visibility, etc. Additionally, the forecaster may be able to direct your attention to any potential hazards, and will almost certainly be able to tell you about the likely changes within the next twenty-four hours or so.

Such forecasts are obviously of great use but, unfortunately, you cannot guarantee to get one on every occasion. On potentially good days in popular areas, the telephone lines are often jammed with people wanting forecasts. In any event, even the professionals can get it wrong every now and then (although not so often as is commonly thought). It therefore makes sense to have at least a working knowledge of weather systems and their effects.

MAJOR AIRSTREAMS
One of the reasons that Britain gets such a wide variety of weather is its geographical position. Situated between a large ocean and a continental land mass, it is at the junction of two large masses of air, one cold and dry, originating from the polar regions, the other warm and moist, coming from the tropics. These air masses mix and slowly divide into airstreams, six of which have an affect on our weather (Fig. 25). If you know which airstream is affecting the country, you will have an idea of the general weather conditions which can be expected.

The most common airstream, affecting the country for over one third of the year, is the polar maritime which originates from Canada and comes to us from the west or north-west. It typically results in cool weather, with heavy and prolonged showers in the mountains. Occasionally polar maritime air can travel into the Atlantic where it swirls around a depression (See page 133) and approaches Britain from the south-west. In this case it will bring warm, cloudy weather, possibly with squally showers.

Next in order of frequency is the tropical maritime airstream

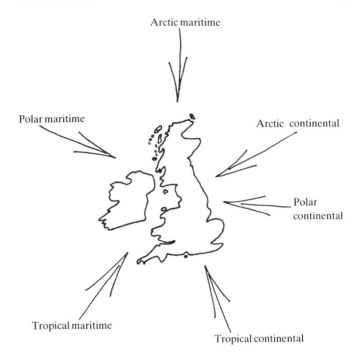

Fig. 25. Airstreams affecting the British Isles

which comes over the Atlantic from the south-west. In summer it gives warm weather with the possibility of low stratus cloud over the western mountains. In winter it results in very mild, moist conditions, often with total cloud cover.

Polar continental air comes from Siberia, reaching Britain from the east. It tends to be hot and hazy in summer, and bitterly cold in winter.

The tropical continental airstream is extremely rare. It originates from Africa, and blows up from the south giving heat-wave weather with possible thunder.

Arctic air can also affect Britain. Arctic maritime air blows from the north, originating from the Arctic Ocean. In summer it gives surprisingly cold weather with frequent heavy and prolonged showers. In winter it can bring heavy snowfall to Scotland and Snowdonia. Arctic continental, like polar continental, blows from the east, but comes from northern Russia. Blowing only in winter it gives extremely severe, bitingly cold, windy weather.

DEPRESSIONS AND FRONTAL SYSTEMS
When airstreams of different character meet, they tend to become unstable. Small ripples occur which can lead to swirling depressions or lows. Whilst it is not necessary for you to know the complexities of their formation, it is important that you understand the ways in which they can affect the weather.

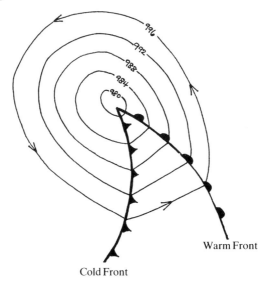

Fig. 26. Frontal system. A typical depression or 'low' and associated frontal system. Note the wind swirls around the low in an anticlockwise direction

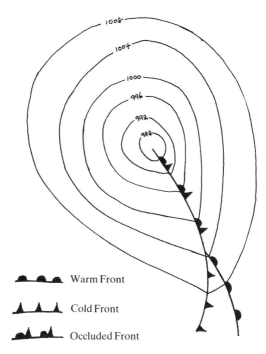

Fig. 27. Occluded Front. Here the Cold Front has caught up with the Warm Front to form an Occluded Front

A depression is an area of low atmospheric pressure. Pressure is shown on a weather map by a series of lines, isobars, which work in exactly the same way as contour lines. The closer the contour lines, the steeper will be the angle of slope; the closer the isobars, the stronger will be the wind.

The junction between two airstreams is known as a front. If warm air is advancing, the junction is known as a warm front whereas if cold air is advancing, it is known as a cold front. Both fronts occur in a depression, the warm front usually ahead of the cold, and the whole system tends to move in a general easterly direction at speeds of between twenty and eighty kilometres an hour (Fig. 26). However, cold fronts tend to move faster than warm fronts, eventually catching them up and forcing the warm air off the ground to form an occluded front (Fig. 27).

Depressions and frontal systems can cause changes in the weather as they pass over the mountains. Luckily there are ways of predicting (more or less) how the weather will change. This must be done by studying the wind and, more importantly, the clouds.

Wind speed and direction can be affected by the local topography (See section 2.4), judgements relying on wind direction must therefore be made with care. Assuming that the topography has not altered the direction of the wind to any great extent, the general rule is that if you stand with your back to the wind, the depression will be to your left.

As the depression advances towards you the wind will begin to increase in speed and change its heading in an anticlockwise direction (Fig. 28). This anticlockwise change of direction is known

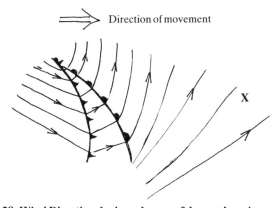

Direction of movement

X

Fig. 28. Wind Direction during advance of depression. A person standing at point **X** would experience a slow 'backing' of the wind as the depression approached, followed by two successive 'veerings' as each front passed

as backing. As the warm front passes, the wind will suddenly veer or change direction clockwise, as it will also when the cold front comes along. If the front has occluded, there will obviously be only one sudden directional change, even though the wind will continue to veer after the front has passed. Generally speaking, a backing wind warns of worsening weather whereas a veering wind promises better conditions in the future.

Frontal systems bring with them a typical succession of clouds and weather, which can be used to track the advance of depressions and to predict future changes. For this reason it is vitally important that you learn to recognize the various cloud types.

Referring to Fig. 29, the first signs of a frontal system are usually cirrus clouds which can form at any time between ten and twenty-four hours in advance of the warm front. Cirrus clouds can come in various forms; the banded mare's tails, possibly moving fairly rapidly, are the precursor to a warm front.

The cirrus cloud slowly develops into cirrostratus, continuous high, wispy sheets which cast haloes around the sun or moon. These soon thicken and lower into grey altostratus which may give the first few drops of rain.

The closer the approach of the warm front, the lower and darker will be the cloud, eventually forming a continuous, low, dark sheet of stratus or nimbo-stratus, the latter giving rain.

The warm front usually brings a belt of steady rain which eases and becomes intermittent as the front passes. The wind suddenly veers and decreases in strength, the temperature rises, and the clouds may start to break up and form stratocumulus with a few

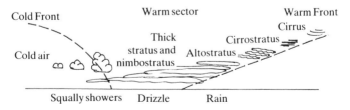

Fig. 29. Weather and clouds associated with passing frontal system

sunny intervals. However, in mountain areas, the warm sector between the warm and cold fronts often contains low and continuous cloud, giving poor visibility and intermittent rain or drizzle.

As the cold front approaches, the wind will begin to strengthen again, and cumulus clouds will begin to form. In mountain regions, these will often be hidden by lower cloud sheets. At the cold front itself there are often towering cumulonimbus clouds giving sudden squalls and heavy showers which may be thundery and of hail. The wind will suddenly veer and, because of the advancing band of cold air, the temperature will drop dramatically.

Once the cold front has passed there will usually be a marked improvement in the weather. The temperature will stay low, but the rain will become more showery and the skies will start to clear, leaving the odd cumulus.

If the fronts have occluded by the time they reach you, the sequence will remain essentially the same except there will be no rise of temperature and no warm sector, the sequence jumping straight from the belt of steady rain to the clearing skies. The change in the direction of the wind is also usually far greater than would otherwise be the case. Statistically, most cyclonic rain which falls on Britain is associated with occluded fronts.

ANTICYCLONIC WEATHER

British weather is not only affected by depressions or lows, but also by anticyclones – areas of high pressure. In many ways the two pressure systems tend to be total opposites. Generally speaking anticyclones, tend to be slow-moving, giving reasonably settled weather, often with low winds and clear skies. Temperature inversions are common under these conditions (See section 2.3).

There are two main types of anticyclonic weather which we experience in Britain: the ridge of high pressure, and the blocking high.

A ridge of high pressure can be identified from a weather map in exactly the same way as a topographical ridge can be identified from a normal map. These ridges are fairly common, passing relatively quickly across the country to give good weather for a few days.

However, the clear night skies which are usually associated with them may bring fog and surprisingly cold weather to mountain valleys.

A blocking high is a very large, extremely slow-moving area of high pressure which can sit over Britain (or western Europe) and divert depressions away from their normal course. In summer, such highs lead to hot, dry, settled weather, the incredible heat wave of 1976 being a good example. If the blocking high is not directly over the country, it can lead to good conditions in one area at the expense of another.

In winter, a blocking high is a totally different proposition. Far from bringing unseasonably warm weather, it can cause extremely cold air to whistle across the country, often with strong easterly winds.

We have now dealt, albeit briefly, with the main causes of the weather which occurs in the British mountains. Those of you who are interested enough to delve more deeply will find details of further reading in Appendix II. With practice and experience, you should be able to use the knowledge you have gained not only to modify the general weather forecast, but also, and perhaps more importantly, to recognize potential, unpredicted changes when you are actually on the hill.

It is of little use knowing what is going to happen to the weather unless you know how the conditions will affect you. Like everything else to do with mountaincraft, you must get practical experience of conditions and their effects. Be observant when you are out: watch the clouds and note the changes in wind speed and direction, see how various conditions affect your performance or safety. It is only by the observation of practical situations that you will become weatherwise.

Part three

Human conditions

3.1 **Introduction**

In this part of the book we will be concerned with a variety of human conditions, most of which are caused either directly or indirectly by inclement weather (see Part two). They are all avoidable. In addition to a section on mountain hypothermia, a condition which is probably the most insidious of all mountain hazards, we will look at the ways in which extremes of both heat and cold can affect the body. There is also a section on benightment, another devoted to a number of minor ailments, and a final discussion about the basics of mountaineering first aid.

Before looking at these conditions in detail, it is perhaps desirable to take another look at attitude (See section 1.2), in itself a form of human condition.

For the vast majority of people, an atmosphere of adventure is a vitally important part of all mountain activities. If we accept (as we surely must) that risk is an essential ingredient of adventure, it follows that the vast majority of people take risks when they go into the hills. Whilst I agree that, put this way, the statement is somewhat contentious, it is nevertheless true. The crux of the matter is whether the risks can be justified by the person taking them.

I know a hill walker who refuses to go rock climbing. He says he finds it too dangerous. What he means is that he cannot justify the personal risk he finds in rock climbing. However, this same person will quite happily wander around the hills by himself in conditions which would cause one of my climbing acquaintances to retreat rapidly in the direction of the nearest hostelry. Although he is a bold rock athlete, severe weather poses a risk which he cannot justify to himself. Neither view is wrong; neither the walker nor the climber is any better than the other. Quite simply, each has a different idea of what constitutes an acceptable risk.

In the same way as there are different types of risk, there are different types of adventure. Note that I have deliberately avoided saying that there are different levels of adventure. What some people consider to be a tame walk through a mountain valley may, to others, be a highpoint in their walking lives. Similarly, a rock climb which one person uses as an unroped descent route may prove to be a test piece for someone else. Who is to say which of these views is correct? Who can say which experience is the more adventurous?

Whilst a philosophical discussion of the whys and wherefores of mountain activities is way beyond the scope of this book, it is important to realize that different people have different levels of acceptable or justifiable risk. Your attitude should reflect this realization. If you climb at Hard Very Severe standard, spare a thought for the trembling, white-faced person on the V Diff which you are using as a descent route. He may be more gripped than you would be soloing an Extreme; he certainly will be if you climb all over him and disappear in a cloud of chalk dust.

Some walkers are not blameless in this respect, either. When you arrive back at base, fresh and buoyant after your thirty kilometre stroll over the tops, try not to take the wind from the sails of the exhausted, limping wreck who is beaming with the achievement and adventure of a five kilometre slog through the valley.

Although the arrogance of the excellent can sometimes be met, it is not so much a hazard as an annoyance, spoiling what would otherwise have been a superb day on the hill. The overconfidence of the inexperienced, on the other hand, is a totally different matter, and can only be regarded as a hazard. One problem faced by all people when they start mountain activities is that until they have either directly or indirectly experienced a particular situation, they are unlikely to have sufficient information with which to decide whether or not it represents a risk (See section 1.3). As their experience grows, and they achieve each goal without mishap, it is important that they do not become blasé about the hazards. A

Climbing on the Great Slab, Cwm Silyn. To some people this is foolhardy; to others it is exhilarating. Who can say which opinion is correct?

person with a little experience and a blasé attitude is probably one of the most dangerous things you will ever meet in the mountains, especially if he's holding your rope.

Overconfidence can strike at the experienced just as easily as at the inexperienced. A good example is the common, but mistaken, belief that however easy or difficult you find a particular climb or walk on the first attempt, you will find it easier on the second. Although this may be true of a few technical rock climbs (where knowledge of the location of holds or of the the technique required to pass a section can make a vast difference), generally speaking you will find the second attempt little different to the first.

One final point which should be considered is that mood can have a marked affect on your performance. If you feel good, you usually perform well – and vice versa. Like the chicken and the egg, it is difficult to know which precedes which. There is no doubt, however, that we all have off days when nothing seems to go right. Despite rumours to the contrary, these off days are not caused solely by over indulgence, but seem to occur without rhyme or reason. As with all other factors, if you are having a bad day, even when there seems to be no logical explanation, do not be afraid to modify your plans.

3.2 Mountain hypothermia

Make no mistake about it: mountain hypothermia is a killer. There are a number of reasons for this, not all of which are medical. It can be very difficult to diagnose the approach of the condition, so it often creeps up on parties, catching them unawares. Even when it is diagnosed early there can still be problems, for the period of time between its onset and death can be remarkably short. Owing to the number of variables involved, every incidence of the condition is unique, and it is therefore impossible to give any average or typical times. However, it would not be an exaggeration to say that death

Shelter from the wind is extremely important, especially whenever you stop for a break. Note the poor visibility in the background due to spindrift.

has been known to occur within two hours of onset.

Despite a considerable amount of publicity by such organizations as the British Mountaineering Council, the mechanisms of the condition are still misunderstood by a surprisingly large number of people. This is a great shame, for not only is mountain hypothermia avoidable, but even when it does occur, prompt action can usually prevent death.

You will remember that in section 1.4 we said it would be helpful to think of the human body as consisting of two separate parts: the core (containing all the vital organs), and the shell (surrounding and protecting them). It was also noted that, being warm blooded, we must maintain a certain temperature if we are to operate efficiently. As far as hypothermia is concerned, it is the temperature of the core which is critical. If heat loss is allowed to exceed heat production, the temperature of the core will begin to fall.

WINDCHILL

Windchill is a term commonly used when talking about mountain hypothermia. There is nothing complicated or magical about it, it simply refers to the chilling effect of the wind. Still air usually has a cooling effect because its ambient temperature is less than the temperature of the core (normally 37°C). If the air moves, even if by only a small amount as in a breeze, it will increase its cooling effect. The lower wind speeds have the greatest influence on the temperature, thus slow moving air has a relatively greater cooling effect than fast moving air. A typical windchill table is shown in Fig. 30.

Whilst tables like this are useful, they do not tell the full story, for moisture has an extremely important part to play. In section 1.4 we saw that wet clothing can conduct about 250 times as much heat away from the body as dry clothing, and that evaporation (which is enhanced by moving air) can lead to massive heat loss. Although the vast majority of heat loss can be controlled simply by wearing the correct clothing, it is important that you understand the effects of windchill, for even if the ambient temperature seems acceptable, the windchill temperature can be well below freezing. A graphic example of this is the fact that frost-nip can occur when the air

Wind speed (kph)	Ambient temperature (thermometer reading) (°C.)						
	12	8	4	0	−4	−8	−12
0	12	8	4	0	−4	−8	−12
10	8	5	0	−4	−8	−13	−17
20	4	0	−5	−10	−15	−21	−26
30	0	−3	−8	−14	−20	−25	−31
40	−1	−5	−11	−17	−23	−29	−35
50	−2	−6	−12	−18	−25	−31	−37
60	−4	−7	−13	−19	−26	−32	−39
70	−4	−7	−14	−20	−27	−33	−40

Fig. 30. Windchill Chart

temperature is above freezing (See section 3.4). The majority of mountain hypothermia cases occur when the ambient temperature is between 5°C and 10°C.

EXHAUSTION

There are a number of other factors which must be considered, the most important of which is exhaustion. We have already seen that a considerable amount of energy is used when mountain walking or climbing, and that this energy needs to be made available through food (See sections 1.5 and 1.6). A diet which provides 4000 kilocalories of daily energy should be regarded as the absolute minimum, and high energy snacks should be eaten when on the hill. However, it is no good eating all this food if you do not drink enough, for water is required in the reaction which converts food into energy. So far as energy production is concerned, dehydration will have a similar effect to not eating.

If energy demands exceed energy intake, either because you have eaten insufficient food or because you have attempted too much, your body will begin to use reserve energy which it stores as fat. Apart from the fact that it is bad practice to rely on stored energy in this way (you never know when an emergency may require that little bit of extra effort), it takes time for stored energy to be released. If you are losing heat rapidly, the energy that is being released may be insufficient to maintain your body temperature. Exhaustion, therefore, can play a major part in the onset of mountain hypothermia, and can cause it to occur in weather conditions which might otherwise be thought quite mild.

SHOCK
People who have had an accident and are suffering from shock may be unable to produce enough energy to maintain their body temperature. They will be immobile and so will not be producing heat via muscular work. It is therefore vitally important that you minimize their heat loss.

INDIVIDUAL FACTORS
Although the mechanisms are not fully understood, there is no doubt that psychology plays an important part in the onset of mountain hypothermia. It appears that those people who have thought about the effects of inclement weather and the possibilities of benightment (See section 3.5) are better equipped to survive than those who have not. Moreover, walking parties with low morale appear to be more susceptible to hypothermia than those who are cheerful. As strange as it may seem, cheerful, well-read people with a calm disposition have a greater tolerance to mountain hypothermia than others.

Body chemistry may also have a large part to play, for various chemicals produced within the body can affect such things as the production of heat, the conversion of food into energy, the rate of heartbeat, and the amount of blood flow to the shell. Using the process of vaso-constriction, the body can reduce the amount of blood flow to the shell in an attempt to reduce heat loss (See section 2.3). However, adrenalin, a body chemical produced to help in times of stress to aid either 'fight or flight', has the effect of increasing both the heart-rate and the flow of blood through the capillaries. This means it can literally reverse the effects of vaso-constriction, causing warm blood from the core to flow into the cold shell. The consequences of this can be extremely serious, for the result will be a sudden flow of cool blood into the core.

The avoidance of mountain hypothermia therefore tends to be reliant upon a number of factors, including adequate clothing, sufficient intake of food, and good morale. Additionally, people recovering from illness can be more susceptible to cold, as can those taking certain drugs. Nevertheless, if one member of a party is suffering from the condition, it is wise to assume that everyone else is nearing the danger level.

URGENCY OF TREATMENT

It may be stating the obvious, but it is important to realize that the longer the heat loss continues, the colder the core temperature will become, and the more serious will be the effect. If the core temperature drops below about 35°C, it may be impossible for the body to recover by itself, even if the heat loss is stopped. Additionally, if the condition continues for any length of time, the various chemical changes which will have occurred in the body may cause severe problems. Unless hospitalized and under medical supervision, these problems may be serious enough to result in death on rewarming. It is therefore vitally important that the condition is treated at the earliest possible opportunity. However, there is a problem: the condition can be extremely difficult to diagnose until it has become severe.

STAGES AND SYMPTOMS

For the purpose of clarity, I have divided symptoms into a number of stages, each of which is associated with a drop in core temperature. It must be made perfectly clear, however, that things are not so straightforward in the field, some victims displaying different symptoms to those indicated, others displaying similar symptoms but in a different order. Generally speaking, if the weather conditions are bad, any irrational or strange behaviour should be regarded as being indicative of hypothermia.

The first stage, which we will call mild hypothermia, occurs as the core temperature starts to drop towards 35°C. The victim, who will be feeling cold and tired and may have been complaining of cramp, will find that his natural response to cold (i.e. shivering) becomes uncontrollable. This will reach a peak at about 35°C. As his core temperature drops, lethargy will increase, and he will start to become withdrawn and apathetic. His limbs will start to become numb as vaso-constriction reduces the blood supply to a trickle, and this will lead to fumbling and a general lack of co-ordination. In very cold conditions, it will also increase the chances of frost-bite (See section 3.4).

Provided the heat loss is stopped, it is possible for sufferers of mild hypothermia to recover without additional help. The situation becomes far more serious as the core temperature drops from 35°C to 31°C. We will call this next stage moderate hypothermia. The most insidious aspect of the condition will now begin to make itself felt, for the victim will refuse to acknowledge he has a problem, and may even become violent if you try to help him. By this time, vaso-constriction will be so great that all shivering will have ceased, movements will have become sluggish or erratic, and muscles will have become stiff. Stumbling will increase, and it will take more and more effort for the victim to recover from falls. Due to the lack of blood in his shell, he will probably look fairly pale.

At about 33°C, the drop in core temperature will begin to affect seriously the workings of the vital organs, particularly the brain. The victim will certainly be irrational, probably incoherent, and could start suffering from amnesia. It is not unknown for victims to become convinced that they are too warm and start taking off their clothes. The visual cortex appears to be particularly vulnerable during this phase; difficulty in focusing, hallucinations, and other forms of visual abnormality commonly occur.

People suffering from moderate hypothermia will need help in order to recover. Not only will they be unable to do anything for themselves (indeed, as we have seen, they may not even recognize that they are in danger), but also simply stopping further heat loss will be insufficient to prevent a worsening of the condition, for the core temperature will have affected the vital functions to such an extent that the body will be unable to reverse the cooling effect. External heat is therefore needed if the patient is to survive.

If the core temperature drops below 31°C, the victim will enter a critical phase which we will call severe hypothermia. Both pulse and respiration will start to weaken, and the degree of stupor will increase. The skin of severe hypothermics usually takes on a sickly blue-grey tone, and as the core temperature decreases further, so the pupils start to dilate. Below about 30°C the pulse will become irregular and the victim will drift into unconsciousness. Even if the heat loss is stabilized, the victim will die unless medical help reaches him within a few hours.

A further problem with severe hypothermia is that chemical changes occur which will make recovery far more difficult. Indeed, it is essential to have medical supervision during the rewarming of victims of severe hypothermia, because these chemical changes can cause complications which may prove fatal.

If the core temperature drops below 29°C, the victim will enter the acute hypothermic phase in which most reflexes cease to function. The pulse and respiration will continue to weaken and become erratic, and below about 28°C the autonomic nervous system, which controls vital functions such as heartbeat and breathing, will begin to fail. Eventually there will be no sign of respiration or pulse. It is extremely important that you do not take a lack of pulse or respiration to be a sign of death. Low body temperatures will reduce the need for oxygen, and there have been documented cases where acutely hypothermic casualties have made total recoveries after having exhibited no pulse or respiratory action for over an hour. Artificial respiration and cardiac compression should therefore be given to acute hypothermics who are apparently dead, and the treatment should be continued until the arrival of medically qualified help (See section 3.7).

TREATMENT
There is little use in being able to recognize hypothermia unless one knows how to treat it. It is important you appreciate that the victim may deny he has problems, especially if he has reached the stage of moderate hypothermia. He may become abusive or even violent when you try to help him, but you must persevere, for if he has reached this stage, he will be dead within a few hours without your help. Whatever phase the victim has reached, prompt action is a

prime requirement of the successful treatment of mountain hypothermia.

If you know what to look for and you know your companions reasonably well, you should be able to diagnose the onset of even mild hypothermia fairly quickly. When this happens, the immediate need is for shelter, especially from the wind. Do not, at this stage, attempt to reach the valley floor; any expenditure of energy on the part of the victim could cause a further drop in core temperature with possibly fatal consequences.

When you have found (or made) some form of shelter, get the victim out of his wet clothes and into dry, spare clothing (See section 1.4), put him inside a survival bag, and insulate him from the ground with rucksacks, sleep-mats, or whatever else is available. Once this has been done, you must try to warm him in some way. If you have a sleeping bag available, so much the better, but get someone else to warm the bag first; the victim's skin temperature will probably be so low that he will be unable to warm a cold sleeping bag, and it will therefore have little effect. If no sleeping bag is available, a companion should share his body warmth by lying in the survival bag with the casualty.

Once this has been done, hot drinks (either freshly made or from a flask) plus some easily digestible, high energy food will be a great help. No matter how anxious you are, reassure the casualty, smile, keep calm, and try to keep up morale. Reassurance (known in America as TLC – Tender Loving Care) is extremely important, and can make all the difference between recovery and deterioration.

If treatment is started promptly, there is every chance that the victim will recover. This, however, will take time (usually well over an hour), during which period the rest of the party will be left doing very little. This inactivity could, in itself, lead to more people becoming hypothermic. Make sure all the people involved (including yourself) put on extra clothing, stay out of the wind, and have something hot to drink. This is the time to open your emergency rations (See section 1.5), and if you have prepared them in the way suggested, the resulting fun and hilarity as you try to break your way past yards of sticky tape can be used as a great morale booster.

Recovery, if and when it does occur, can not only be rapid, but can also appear to be total. Even if this is the case, on no account should you attempt to carry on, for the ex-victim will have been severely weakened by his experience. If you are sure that the victim has recovered, you must find the easiest way off the mountain. Do not forget that the easiest way will not necessarily be the quickest. If recovery does not occur within two hours, or if conditions worsen, the victim should be treated as a moderate hypothermic (See below).

It is important that you understand what you are doing and why. Although the essential part of any treatment is to stop all further heat loss, you must be extremely careful not to warm the shell to such an extent that vaso-constriction is suddenly reversed. This could happen, for example, as a result of massage, vigorous rubbing, or intense local warming. If this occurs, warm core blood will flow to the shell whilst the cold shell blood will quickly flow to the core. Such an effect could easily kill. It is for this reason that alcohol should not be given to anyone in poor weather conditions, for one of the many effects of alcohol is to dilate the capillaries, thus increasing the flow of blood to the shell. If you understand the mechanisms of hypothermia, you will understand how dangerous this could be.

A victim of moderate hypothermia is in a dangerous condition and any further heat loss could prove fatal. Unless you can find shelter from the elements, you will have to think very carefully before removing their wet clothes, for even these will have a certain insulation value (albeit minimal) and will contain a small amount of heat. Removal will therefore cause an overall heat loss. If you decide not to remove the clothes, the victim should immediately be placed inside a survival bag, and further insulation in the form of sleeping bags or dry clothes should be wrapped around him, the whole thing possibly being covered by a further survival bag. Do not forget the essential insulation between the victim and the ground.

Sufferers of moderate hypothermia are unable to recover by themselves. In order to get their core temperature back to normal, they need a source of external heat. In the mountains, this is often supplied by a companion who lies alongside the victim in order to share bodily warmth. The problem is that, to be of any use, there should be skin to skin contact in the area of the chest. This is obviously not possible unless the victim's wet clothes are removed, but removing them may cause further heat loss. There is no easy way around this paradox.

The dilemma may be partly solved if the victim remains conscious or if the group are carrying a tent. In the former instance, the heat balance is helped by the administration of hot, sweet drinks (never attempt to give drinks to unconscious victims). If the party has a tent, this should be pitched and the victim carried inside. As many members of the party as possible should then get inside with him in order to raise the temperature. Alternatively, if you have a stove which can safely be lit inside the tent, so much the better, but beware the risks of fire and of poor ventilation. A large group squeezed into a tent may help morale as long as the victim remains conscious.

The whole point of the exercise is to prevent further heat loss without rapidly increasing the temperature of the shell. If, at the same time, it is possible to warm the victim in some way, then so much the better. Do not forget that the rest of the party will also be cold and tired, and could quite easily become hypothermic. As before, morale and reassurance are extremely important for everyone concerned.

Although it is possible for a victim of moderate hypothermia to recover whilst on the hill, he must be regarded as a stretcher case. Even if he appears to make a total recovery, you will have to summon help (See section 1.7). The self-evacuation of even a moderately hypothermic casualty is a serious undertaking, and the decision to attempt such a task on an improvised stretcher should not be taken lightly. Carrying a casualty is extremely strenuous, and as it is likely that other members of the party are fairly near hypothermia themselves, it is asking for trouble to expect them to accomplish the feat. Far better to sit it out, keeping in shelter and protecting the casualty whilst waiting for the resuce team to arrive.

Unless action is taken to prevent the condition deteriorating to the severe or acute stage, the situation will become very grave indeed. Without wishing to sound overly dramatic, no matter what action is taken by their companions, victims of severe and acute hypothermia will die within a few hours unless they receive medical assistance. All one can do is to prevent further heat loss in an attempt to stabilize the core temperature, and to provide general (*not local*) warming in an effort to reverse the downward trend.

Several other books on mountaincraft mention alternative ways of treating the victim, including hot baths, hot packs, and airway rewarming. These require equipment not usually carried by a party, for example the means to heat fairly substantial quantities of water, or a bath. Airway rewarming, in particular, requires specialist equipment and should only be done by persons experienced in its use. The other two methods are virtually impossible to use on the hill, with the possible exception of the hot pack, which may be found useful on those rare occasions when a party has been able to evacuate the victim to a bothy. If you require further information about these methods of treatment, you will find various sources listed in Appendix II.

It may sound trite, but the best way to deal with mountain hypothermia is to avoid it. However, even if you do everything right yourself, you may come across someone else who is suffering from the condition. If you do meet it on the hill, you will inevitably find that the situation is not at all clear cut, and you will probably be faced with a number of extremely difficult decisions.

There is no such thing as a textbook case of mountain hypothermia – every incident is unique and requires its own treatment to effect a recovery. All you can do is remember the mechanisms of the condition: that hypothermia is caused by heat loss; that the temperature of the core must be stabilized or increased; that local warming or stimulation of the periphery will cause a sudden, possibly fatal drop in the temperature of the core; and that the victim must be allowed to rest in order to recover.

3.3 Heat stroke

It is not only an overall heat loss which causes problems to the human system. Any imbalance between heat loss and heat gain is serious and will eventually lead to death if allowed to continue unchecked. Uncontrolled heat loss (or hypothermia) is by far the most common form of imbalance, but uncontrolled heat gains can also occur on hot days in summer. The most severe manifestation of overheating is heat stroke, a condition which can prove fatal.

HEAT CONTROL MECHANISMS

The heat-control mechanisms of the body have already been discussed in a number of sections. In cold conditions, the body reduces heat loss by decreasing the blood flow to the shell by means of vaso-constriction. In hot conditions, the converse applies, and heat loss is intensified by increasing the peripheral blood flow by means of vaso-dilation, an effect which results in a corresponding increase in the rate of sweat production.

Under normal circumstances, the cooling of the blood as it flows near the surface of skin, which has itself been cooled by the evaporation of sweat, is sufficient to offset the effects of raised temperatures and thus maintain the heat balance. However, all muscular activity produces heat, and the intense activity undertaken in strenuous mountain walking or climbing may overload the system, causing the body to gain heat faster than it can lose it. It is at this stage that problems begin.

As the body starts to overheat, there is a dramatic increase in the production of sweat in an attempt to cool the skin. Often this will redress the balance, but the increased sweat production makes severe demands upon the body's reserves of salt and water. If sweating at this level continues for any length of time, the body will begin to suffer from salt deficiency. This will result in the first stage of heat stroke, known as heat cramp.

HEAT CRAMP

Heat cramp is extremely painful. It usually occurs in the muscles of the legs and abdomen, and the condition can be exacerbated by the effects of vaso-dilation. Indeed, the capillaries may have dilated to such an extent that there is less blood than usual in the brain, and this can lead to light-headedness and a general feeling of weakness.

The condition should be taken as a warning that heat stroke is looming on the horizon. Treatment should therefore be immediate.

The first requirement is for some form of shade. If there is no natural shade in the vicinity, you will be forced to construct some. A survival bag can be extremely useful for this purpose. Once this has been done, the victim should be allowed to rest, and should be given plenty of water in which there is a little salt. Two pinches of salt per litre is perfectly adequate; at greater concentrations the liquid becomes emetic. Alternatively, salt tablets can be taken, or you can use one of the fruit-flavoured electrolyte-replacement drinks. Cramp can be eased by stretching and massaging the affected muscles.

Assuming that salt and shade are available, recovery is usually fairly rapid. If this is so, the victim should be led slowly off the hill by the easiest (and coolest) route. He should not be allowed to exert himself unnecessarily, and there certainly should be no question of his continuing the planned activity.

HEAT EXHAUSTION

If the level of sweating continues, not only will there be a salt deficiency, but there will also be danger of dehydration. Further physical exertion could cause the core temperature to rise, the result almost certainly being heat exhaustion – a far more serious condition.

The symptoms of heat exhaustion are an extension of those of heat cramp, but without the cramp. The victim, who will most likely be sweating profusely as the body vainly tries to lose heat, will complain of nausea, headache, fatigue and light-headedness. His pulse and respiration may increase as more and more blood flows into the capillaries, and his skin will often feel cold and clammy. He may faint and vomit.

The treatment is essentially the same as that for heat cramp, except that the liquid should only be given in sips as the victim will be nauseated by it. Once he is in some form of shade, it will help to loosen or even remove any unnecessary clothing. Whereas in cases of hypothermia one must reduce heat loss by keeping the victim warm, in heat exhaustion one must try to increase heat loss by keeping the victim cool. When he has cooled sufficiently for the nausea to disappear, further liquid should be given in an attempt to offset the effects of dehydration. If salt tablets or electrolyte-replacement drinks are available, then so much the better.

It will take far longer for a person to recover from heat exhaustion than from heat cramp, and it is vitally important that he is allowed plenty of time in which to rest in relatively cool conditions before being escorted off the hill. Heat exhaustion has a nasty habit of recurring, and can all too easily become heat stroke. This is an extremely serious condition, and victims should be regarded as being critically ill.

HEAT STROKE
In heat stroke, the core temperature has increased to such an extent that the mechanisms of vaso-dilation and sweating begin to break down. To put it more simply, the body becomes unable to lose heat. As a result of this, the core temperature will continue to rise and the victim will die within a very short period of time. Heat stroke can be precipitated from heat exhaustion in humid conditions simply because the sweat will not evaporate quickly enough.

Like hypothermia, heat stroke is caused by a breakdown of the core temperature, and the symptoms are initially very similar. As well as showing the symptoms of heat exhaustion, the victim will probably become irrational or aggressive. Confusingly, his skin may either be hot red and dry, or cool pale and damp. His core temperature will be in excess of 41°C, and if this is not reduced extremely quickly, the victim will go into convulsions and die.

The body temperature must be decreased *immediately*. It is insufficient simply to place the victim in some shade; you should actively reduce his temperature by removing clothing and vigorously fanning. Where possible, damp clothes or, better still, cool water should be applied to his head and neck to promote further cooling. If he is conscious, or if he regains consciousness, he should be reassured and given sips of water.

Heat stroke victims should be regarded as stretcher cases even on those rare occasions when they appear to make a complete recovery. Once off the hill, it is imperative that they get medical advice as soon as possible.

Do not forget that heat cramp, heat exhaustion and heat stroke are all related, and can be regarded as progressive stages of the same ailment. In simple terms, their underlying cause is that heat gain begins to exceed heat loss. If you understand this principle, you will recognize that it is possible to suffer from heat exhaustion on a cool day when you are over clothed and under ventilated, and involved in particularly strenuous activity.

AVOIDANCE
All three stages are avoidable, even in the hottest of weathers. The key is not only adequate liquid, but also common sense: anyone who toils up a mountain in heavy clothing on a hot day is asking for trouble. As with so many other hazards, avoidance is ninety per cent common sense, ten per cent knowledge.

WATER
It is of little use having enough water with you unless you drink it. Water requirements were discussed in section 1.5, and it was mentioned that it is best to drink little and often. Apart from the fact that drinking large quantities of liquid can make you feel uncomfortable, it can also give you stomach cramp. In hot weather, in particular, you should drink at regular intervals, whether you feel thirsty or not.

SALT
Some people need extra salt in their diets during hot weather, but it is not generally necessary. Salt tablets are useful for emergencies and should be kept in your first-aid kit, but I cannot recommend their use at any other time. If you feel you need some extra salt (your muscles will soon tell you if you do), you will be better advised to buy some of the fruit-flavoured electrolyte salts which are available nowadays from many mountaineering equipment shops.

3.4 **Frost-bite**
In the last section we saw how heat stroke is the final stage in a progression which starts with heat cramp. Frost-bite, too, can be regarded as a progressive condition. In its mildest form it is known

as frost-nip. If left untreated, this can progress to superficial frost-bite, and ultimately to deep frost-bite. Although the latter is a rare occurrence in the British mountains, frost-nip is more common than is generally imagined, and superficial frost-bite should be considered a major hazard during any emergency situation in winter. All stages are avoidable.

Frost-bite is initiated by a reduction in the flow of blood to the extremities. This is usually, though not always, caused by vaso-constriction (See section 1.4). In addition to carrying nutrients, blood also carries warmth, and as the blood-flow becomes more sluggish, the surrounding tissue will begin to cool. If the environmental temperature is cold enough, the flesh of the extremities can literally freeze, and ice crystals will form in between the cells. If allowed to continue, this situation can cause cells to rupture and die. Once this has happened, infection is a very real problem.

The areas most commonly affected are the toes, fingers, ears, nose, and cheeks.

FROST-NIP

The first stage of frost-bite is known as frost-nip, and indicates that the tissue has begun to freeze. If, having felt cold or painful, your hands or feet become numb, you should suspect frost-nip. Sometimes the cold or numbness is replaced by a paradoxical feeling of warmth – do not be misled. A further, fairly easily identifiable symptom when the area is visible is that the flesh begins to look like white candle-wax. You may see this on your companions' nose, cheeks or ears, possibly before they realize the problem.

The treatment of frost-nip is simple and effective; the affected part must be rewarmed. On no account should you rub it. Cheeks, ears and nose usually present few problems as they can be rewarmed by the hands. Fingers can be placed under the armpits, preferably beneath one or two layers of clothing. Toes present more

Ice on the hills. You do not need snow to get conditions in which frost-nip is a potential hazard.

of a problem, and require the help of another person. The normal procedure is to remove boots and stocking and place the feet under a companion's anorak, using him as a hot-water bottle. The best positions are either under the arms or in the crutch, or if this is too restricting, on the stomach. It is in situations like this that you find out who your friends are! If you suspect you have frost-nipped feet, do not press on regardless simply because it is too much bother to stop, remove boots and stockings, and inspect for signs of damage. Such apathy could lead to serious problems at a later stage.

Recovery from frost-nip may be accompanied by pins-and-needles, tingling sensations, stinging, and probably pain. The damage caused, however mild, is likely to leave you with a permanent weakness because tissue that has been subjected to frost-nip seems far more likely to suffer from the condition (and from the cold in general) than tissue that has not, as those who have suffered in the past will no doubt tell you.

SUPERFICIAL FROST-BITE
If the freezing is allowed to continue, superficial frost-bite will be the inevitable result. This is simply a progression of the condition in which further cells are affected, possibly to a deeper level under the skin. As with frost-nip, the flesh will appear pale and waxy, and because the tissue is frozen, it will be like a hard layer covering the soft, unaffected cells. Whilst there may be some superficial pain to begin with, the area will almost certainly become numb and senseless, although some sufferers have reported a sensation of intense cold.

The treatment for superficial frost-bite is essentially the same as that for frostnip – simple rewarming of the affected part. In this instance, however, it is more important to know what not to do. Under no circumstances should you rub or chafe the part in order to stimulate circulation – such action could seriously damage the tissue, making the condition far worse. A common misconception is that frost-bitten areas should be rubbed with snow. Unfortunately this is totally the wrong thing to do, for not only do the ice crystals in snow act as an abrasive on already damaged skin, but any resulting moisture will evaporate from the surface of the flesh, thereby chilling it further.

Rewarming does not necessarily lead to the recovery of frost-bite cases. If feeling and colour do not return to the affected area within about half an hour, you must face the fact that there is little you can do without medical help. In these circumstances it is better to return to the valley with the part still frozen than it is to remain on the hill, fruitlessly trying to recover. On no account should you try to force a recovery by rapid reheating using, for example, a stove or hot water; you are likely to do far more harm than good.

Even if the treatment is effective, and feeling and colour return, great care should be taken to ensure that the affected part is not refrozen, for this will further harm an already weakened area. When the affected part is a toe, far less damage will be caused by walking off the hill with the toe in its frozen state than would be the case if it had been thawed. However, steps should be taken to ensure that the condition does not get any worse, for in deep-seated frost-bite (the ultimate progression) there is a very high risk of permanent damage, with possible loss of tissue.

If the condition goes beyond the stage of frost-nip, you must take the easiest way off the hill and seek medical advice.

EFFECTS OF WINDCHILL
There are a number of circumstances, apart from sub-zero temperatures, in which frost-bite should be considered a possibility. The first occurs on moist or misty days when the wind is fairly fresh and the temperature slightly above freezing point. In these conditions, it is possible for frost-nip to occur due to the fact that the windchill temperature is well below zero (See section 3.2). This means it is theoretically possible for frost-nip to occur at any time of year in the British mountains, especially in the Highlands of Scotland.

DEEP SNOW
Sometimes temperatures can be deceptive. When walking in deep powder snow, for example, the temperature around the legs and feet can be far lower than that of the air. This can have serious results if the feet are not properly protected.

RESTRICTION OF CIRCULATION

Vaso-constriction is not the only cause of sluggish blood flow to the extremities. When we discussed clothing and footwear in section 1.4, it was emphasized that neither should cause any restriction of movement or circulation, especially in winter conditions. The reason for this should now be obvious. Even if your boots fit perfectly in summer, the temptation in winter is to wear an extra pair of socks and cram the feet into the boots. At best, this will result in cold feet; at worst, it will result in frost-bite. You should always be able to wiggle your toes.

The same applies to the fingers. The temptation is to wear several pairs of gloves or mittens, restricting both movement and circulation with obvious dangers. Other things to watch include wearing so many layers above the waist that you restrict the blood flow to the arms, jackets with elasticated cuffs which are too tight, gaiters which restrict the circulation below the knees, and crampon straps which are tied too tightly. Do not make the mistake of thinking that thickness equals warmth whatever the conditions – you will only be warm if the blood can flow freely around the body.

ACCIDENT VICTIMS

Frost-bite presents a serious hazard to victims of mountain hypothermia because of its links with vaso-constriction. It can also strike during an accident where the victim is exhausted, in shock, or has an injured limb. It is unwise to use pneumatic splints on fractured limbs in cold conditions, simply because they may restrict the circulation enough to cause frost-bite.

AVOIDANCE

Avoidance is relatively simple; wear adequate clothing (See section 1.4). Indeed, if you have taken steps to avoid hypothermia, it is unlikely that you will get frost-bitten. However, there are a few other points which may be helpful.

Wet socks and gloves cause a very real danger because they conduct so much body heat away from the flesh; overmitts and gaiters should therefore be regarded as essentials for winter conditions. Touching bare metals or letting your hands get wet with anything which freezes below 0°C (particularly stove fuel) is asking for trouble, for heat will be lost extremely rapidly. Remember also that both alcohol and nicotine are drugs which can make frost-bite more likely.

Finally, it is a good idea to fiddle! If you keep your fingers and toes moving regularly, you will keep the blood flowing and this will prevent the tissue from freezing.

3.5 Benightment

Spending a night in the open on a mountain can be a memorable experience, but unplanned bivouacs are not to be recommended. Particularly in winter, ill-equipped parties will be lucky to survive.

Some experts will tell you that benightment is easily avoided by good planning. Whilst this is undoubtedly true, there will be times when the unexpected happens and your circumstances alter. In addition, simple human nature can intervene. When you go into the mountains to climb it is all too easy to be swayed by the idea that there might just be time to do another route.

Some years ago, I spent a memorable day with a fellow climber on the Great Slab at Cwm Silyn. Although it was early in the season, the weather was superb and we had been moving so well that we decided there was just time for one last route. That was our first mistake. We knew we would not reach the vehicle until after dark, but this did not worry us unduly (second mistake) as we both had headtorches. Decision made, we hid our packs at the base of the climb (third mistake) and set off.

We had chosen the route both for its grade and its name (Sunset Rib, a 330 ft recommended Diff), and we thought we would romp up it without any problem (fourth mistake). Being so early in the year, not only were we slightly out of condition, but we had also misjudged the hours of daylight, and due to problems both with loose rock and poor route-finding, it was dusk by the time we reached the top of the climb. That was when our problems really started: we had not read the guidebook fully (fifth mistake) and did not realize that the climb finished half way up the cliff. We hummed and hahed (sixth mistake) about climbing the recommended continuation, eventually deciding against it, by which time it was too dark find the path which led to the way off.

The descent was a nightmare. Every ledge we followed seemed to end in a precipice, and as the darkness deepened it became more and more difficult to judge depth and size. More than once we rigged the rope for an abseil only to find that the 'big drop' was less than ten feet and easily climbable. By clinging to heather and treading very, very warily we somehow managed to make a scary descent, but by the time we reached the vegetated base of the cliff, we were both cursing the fact that we had left our packs (and therefore our headtorches) below the climb.

Our problems were still not over. Darkness was now well and truly upon us, and each piece of rock looked exactly the same as its neighbour. It took us almost an hour to find our packs and, once found, my companion discovered his headtorch would not work. I will never forget the journey down. Although the path is reasonable, the light from our single headtorch confused us so much that we spent most of the time slipping and scrabbling straight down the scree. Once at the lake, almost 200 metres below the cliff, the situation became a little easier, but we still lost the path on two or three occasions before reaching the good track which led easily to the vehicle.

We were lucky. The story could so easily have ended in tragedy. Not only could we have fallen during the initial descent, but had we become cragfast, we would have had severe problems so early in the season as all our spare kit was at the base of the cliff. The moral of the story is obvious – try not to let your enthusiasm run away with you.

If, for some reason, you find yourself stuck on a mountain after dark, your course of action will depend very much on the state of the party, the time of year, the location, and the weather. Assuming you are properly equipped, it is generally better to stay put unless you are either on a well-defined path, or within easy reach of your destination across known ground. Moving at night across craggy or

Mynydd Llangatwg. The need for a reliable weather forecast and accurate navigation should be obvious from this photograph.

broken ground can be extremely hazardous as it is impossible to
judge depth and distance. Crossing an unknown stream at night can
only be regarded as suicidal (See section 4.8).

MORALE

Ideally, you should always be prepared for a night out. Whilst a
forced bivouac in summer can, in fact, be fun, lack of preparation in
winter can be fatal. Whatever the time of year, whatever the
situation or conditions, once you have decided you are benighted,
you must accept the fact and make the most of it. As with
hypothermia, morale is extremely important, and the people most
likely to survive a winter bivouac are those who have thought about
the problems beforehand.

SHELTER

When faced with unavoidable benightment, try to get as far down
the mountain as is safely possible. This is particularly important in
winter conditions, especially in Scotland. Your main requirement is
shelter from the wind, so if you see any natural shelter as you
descend, stop and use it rather than continue into an area where
there may be none. Rugged areas such as the Cuillins and the
Rhinogs will offer far more natural shelter than more rounded areas
like the Brecon Beacons. For this reason, supposedly gentle
mountains can often be savage in winter.

SNOW SHELTERS

If there is snow on the ground, you may have to build some form of
snow shelter. It is better to use natural shelters than go to the time
and effort of building one yourself. Natural snow holes are often to
be found around rocks or trees (Fig. 31).

Building snow shelters is an exhausting job which takes a long
time even when you have the correct tools. For this reason, not only
should it be done as a last resort, but the decision must be made as
early as possible.

There are basically two alternatives. If the snow is level and
reasonably thick, you can excavate a hole between half a metre and
a metre deep, using the dug snow to form a windbreak. If you can

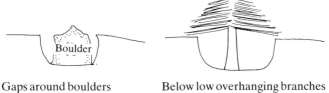

Gaps around boulders

Below low overhanging branches
  of trees

Fig. 31. Natural snow shelters

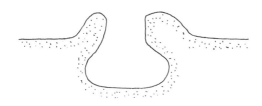

Fig. 32. Snow hole. If you are able to roof this snow hole with
something (spare survival bag, snow 'bricks', etc) it will be far
more effective

roof this over, so much the better (Fig. 32). Trying to do this when
the wind is high and the snow is drifting can be virtually impossible,
but it is precisely in these conditions that you need shelter. Digging
with your hands is not recommended (you are asking for frost-bite);
use your feet, crampons, ice axes, billy cans, or anything else you
can find. Some people consider snow shovels to be essential items of
winter kit.

   If you are near a slope and the snow is of an appreciable depth,
you may be able to dig a snow cave. Although this is probably the
best form of shelter, time will not be on your side, and it is unlikely
that you will be able to construct a textbook snowcave (Fig. 33). It
really does not matter how you do it as long as you get some shelter

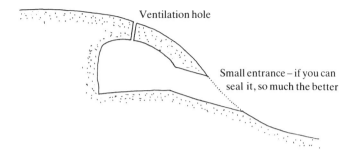

Fig. 33. Snow cave. Note how the main area is higher than the entrance

from the wind. The essential features to remember are a small entrance (start large for ease of access and reduce the size later), some form of ventilation, walls and roof at least three quarters of a metre thick, and the main area higher than the entrance so that warmer air is trapped. The smaller the shelter, the less time it will take to make, and the warmer it will be. Do not forget that you may have to dig your way out of such shelters in the morning, and that it is very easy to lose them if you have to go out during the night.

STRATEGY
Whatever the time of year, once you have found shelter, make yourself as comfortable as possible – it will be a long night. Put on your spare clothing with dry garments next to your skin if possible, loosen your boots (this will help to prevent frost-bite), put your feet inside your rucksack and pull it as far up your legs as possible, get inside your survival bag, and sit on anything (rope, sleep-mat, etc.) which will help to insulate you from the ground (and prevent you from slipping).

This is what your emergency rations are for, so have fun undoing them. Do not be tempted to eat them all at once; remember the rule – little and often. If you can make a brew, so much the better, but be careful if you are in a snow cave. Condensation can soak your clothing where it will then freeze.

It is unlikely that you will get much sleep, and you should deliberately try to stay awake if it is very cold. As you sit there, keep moving various parts of your anatomy in an effort to keep warm, and ensure that the circulation to extremities is not being restricted in any way.

AVOIDANCE

It is best to avoid benightment whenever possible, particularly in winter. There is no special technique involved here; avoidance is simply a matter of descending in time. When planning your route (See section 1.3), allow a little extra time for the unforeseen, and try not only to find suitable escape routes, but also to work out beyond what time they should be used. Do not forget that winter mountain days are very short, especially in Scotland.

One final way of reducing the risk of benightment is to start at the crack of dawn. Here again, we come back to problems of human nature because, judging by the way that many popular car parks fill, most walkers consider dawn to be at about ten o'clock.

3.6 Minor ailments

BLISTERS

Do not underestimate blisters. Not only can they cause great pain, but also, without the correct treatment they may disable the sufferer to such an extent that benightment becomes a real possibility. They can also cause major problems during trips involving camping in wild country. Most mountain enthusiasts have suffered from blisters at some time or other, but although the causes are virtually inevitable, the blister itself is not.

Blisters are caused by the friction of the foot against the boot. This is almost invariably due to one of five reasons: badly fitting or incorrectly laced boots, insufficient or inadequate socks or stockings, foreign bodies, sensitive feet, or simply the fact that you are not used to your boots. Choice of footwear has already been discussed in section 1.4, but however good your boots, it is a fact of life that your feet must get used to walking in them. Although I am on the hill regularly, I still tend to get blisters when I change from winter to summer boots and vice versa – or would do if I did not take evasive action.

Many authorities will tell you to apply surgical spirit to your feet in order to toughen them. Whilst this undoubtedly works for some people, I personally do not like the idea, finding that simple hygiene combined with evasive action at the start of each season is usually sufficient.

Assuming you are not doing anything stupid (like wearing nylon or darned socks, or stumbling around with a piece of grit in your boot), blisters can be avoided easily if you stop immediately you feel a hot spot – the sore area which marks the site of a potential blister. Make sure there is nothing in the sock or boot which is causing the problem (if there is, try to do something about it), then cover the affected area with some form of padding such as plaster, moleskin, or a blister pad. Alternatively, you can use artificial skin – a moist spongy material which feels horrible but works wonderfully. Toes are best covered with micropore bandage used in conjunction with artificial skin. The aim is to reduce the friction which has caused the hot spot.

If a blister has already developed, it is best to burst it gently with a needle which has been sterilized by being held in a flame until red hot. Once the fluid has drained, cover the affected area with artificial skin held in place by micropore or moleskin. If a large area is affected, make sure the moleskin is cut in such a way that it does not form creases.

Once back at base, remove the dressing and let the blister breathe. Make sure your feet are kept clean as this will reduce the chance of infection. If you intend to go walking the next day, cover the area with artificial skin before you set out.

CRAMP
Cramp is a fairly common complaint which can be serious for two reasons: firstly, it is recurrent and can totally immobilize, secondly, it can herald the onset of heat stroke (See section 3.3). It normally occurs in the muscles of the leg, but can also affect the arms during or after strenuous rock climbing.

If the weather is hot or the sufferer has been sweating profusely, you should treat the condition as heat cramp (See section 3.3). In all other cases, relieve the pain by stretching the affected muscle, then head for home.

GLARE
See Snow Blindness.

HEAT SYNCOPE
This is the feeling of lethargy and light-headedness which most people suffer during the first really hot day of the year. It is a common condition and can be severe, leading to acute fatigue and fainting. Caused simply by a lack of acclimatization to heat, it is best treated with rest, preferably in a cool spot.

INSECT BITES AND STINGS
Insect bites are more irritating than dangerous, and prevention is better than treatment. Insect repellent containing diethyltoluamide should be considered if you are particularly sensitive or if you intend to visit a problem area between April and October.

Insect stings are painful, but can be eased in various ways. Wasp stings are the most common, and can be neutralized by the application of an acid substance such as lemon juice. If you have any tobacco with you, spit on the sting and run the tobacco over the site thus releasing nicotinic acid.

Bees usually leave their stings behind. Do not try to pull these out with your fingers as you will only succeed in pumping more poison into your body and pushing the sting further into your flesh. Either leave the sting *in situ* until you return to base, or (better) gently remove it with a sterilized needle. The pain of a bee sting can be eased with an alkaline substance such as bicarbonate of soda, although it is unlikely that you will be carrying this with you on the hill.

Stings are very dangerous when received in the mouth or on a blood vessel. In addition, some people are extremely sensitive and can become seriously ill. Most such sufferers will know of their allergy and will carry suitable medication.

If a person collapses after having been stung, suspect either sensitization or an injected blood vessel. The victim will be in shock, and will have great difficulty in breathing. Try to discover whether the reaction is due to a known allergy and, if so, whether any medication is carried.

When the sting is sited inside the mouth, the subsequent swelling can block the airway. There is very little that can be done except to reduce the swelling as much as possible by immediately getting the victim to take and hold mouthfuls of cold water. You can also place cold compresses outside the throat near the site of swelling.

Generally, if the reaction is bad, there is very little you can do without an antidote. Send for help urgently and try to keep the victim alive until it arrives. Victims need rest, shelter, insulation from the ground, and reassurance. Be alert for heart failure or lack of breathing, and be ready to carry out artificial resuscitation (See section 3.7). It is important that you ensure the rescue team know exactly what has happened so that they can bring the correct drugs with them.

PLASTIC-BOOT ANKLE

A common problem with the larger sizes of many makes of plastic boot is that it is impossible to tie them comfortably around the ankles. On extended trips, this can lead to a painfully sore ring of flesh where the top of the boot rubs. Unless treated, this can become serious – I have seen two cases where the ankle actually blistered.

The treatment is essentially the same as that for blisters, the padding being strapped around the ankle to reduce the friction between it and the top of the boot.

PRICKLY HEAT

Although not a particularly common complaint, prickly heat is both irritating and, in extreme cases, fairly serious. As the name suggests, it occurs in hot weather and is an irritation of the skin caused by tiny blisters which form around blocked sweat glands. In serious cases, the restriction of sweat can affect the body's cooling mechanisms leading to increased risk of heat stroke (See section

3.3). Drinking may produce more sweat which simply makes the situation worse.

If you are unfortunate enough to suffer from this condition, regular cool showers and changes of dry clothing will help. The only real remedy, however, is rest in a cool place.

SNOW BLINDNESS

This condition is so excruciatingly painful that you will not want it to happen twice. The basic problem is that the damage is done before the pain starts, the symptoms slowly appearing between eight and twelve hours afterwards.

Snow blindness is basically sunburn of the eyes, and although not permanent, it can feel as though it is going to last for ever. It is caused by ultra-violet radiation and is easily avoidable. The most serious cases occur during bright snowy days at fairly high altitudes, but similar symptoms can be experienced after a sunny summer day. Contrary to popular belief, it *is* possible to become snow blinded in cloudy conditions.

The symptoms start with a general irritation and dryness which quickly becomes horrendous and feels as if someone has inserted broken glass under the eyelids. Blinking becomes unbelievably painful, the lids swell, and there may be excessive production of tears causing the eyes to water uncontrollably. Even simple exposure to light can cause agony. There is no direct treatment; the condition will heal of its own accord within two or three days. During that time, some of the symptoms can be eased by placing the victim in a darkened room and applying cold compresses to the eyes. Analgesic may be taken for pain, but local anaesthetics should not be given. On no account should the eyes be rubbed. Medical advice should be sought in particularly severe cases.

Luckily, the condition can be easily avoided by wearing suitable sunglasses or goggles. If glasses are worn, they should have some form of patch to prevent light entering around the lenses, for ultra-violet radiation bounces off snow and can therefore enter the eyes from any direction. Some glasses have a patch to stop the nose from being burnt (See sunburn). To be at all effective, the lenses must filter about ninety per cent of the ultra-violet radiation. They

do not necessarily have to be very dark to do this successfully –
indeed, some dark lenses are purely cosmetic and have little
filtering effect.

   If you are caught in bright, snowy conditions without the
necessary protection, particularly during extended trips, you can
improvise protection by cutting a narrow horizontal slit in the card
cover of a map. This is then worn like a pair of snow goggles, being
fixed in place either with a piece of bootlace, or simply by pushing it
under the sides of your anorak hood. Although this will obviously
restrict your vision, it will be far less disabling than snow blindness.

SUNBURN
Although most of us like to try and develop a tan, uncontrolled
sunburn can be extremely serious, and should not be
underestimated. Indeed, acute sunburn is often accompanied by
blistering, and if it affects more than two thirds of the body can
prove fatal. Less acute sunburn can interfere with sweat secretions,
and this can lead to complications resulting in heat stroke (See
section 3.3).

   The easiest way of avoiding sunburn is to wear a good quality
suntan cream (or sunscreen) with a reasonable filter factor. There
are no hard and fast rules about the amount of protection needed
because some people have more sensitive skin than others, but you
will usually need a higher filter factor in the mountains than you
would use on the beach. It is better to use a waterproof sunscreen,
so long as this does not interfere with sweat secretions.

   Sunscreens should be worn in snowy conditions as well as on hot
sunny days. In addition to daubing yourself in all the usual places,
do not forget the earlobes, under the chin, beneath the eyebrows,
and around the nostrils; ultra-violet rays can bounce back from
snowy ground causing painful burns in these areas.

   The lips are best protected with a high-filter-factor lip salve.

3.7 Basic mountaineering first aid

Any accident in the mountains is serious. It is impossible to
telephone for an ambulance or get advice from a doctor, so you

have to rely on your own knowledge and resources. Even if you carry a huge first aid kit containing the latest drugs and dressings, it is of little use unless you know how to use it. A basic knowledge of first aid should therefore be a prime requirement of all mountain enthusiasts.

Personally, I feel that we seriously neglect first aid training in this country. If you want a graphic example of this, ask your immediate friends what they would do if they were in a shopping arcade and someone had a heart attack. The answer 'telephone for an ambulance' is not allowed.

Those injuries normally regarded as being relatively mild can be extremely serious in the mountains because of the remoteness, and you would be well advised to attend a first aid course. Those of you who intend to lead groups will undoubtedly benefit from attending a special mountaineering first aid course. Whatever type you attend, it must be practical, for it is impossible to learn to deal with a fracture or to apply artificial resuscitation from a book.

In the case of first aid, the saying 'a little knowledge is a dangerous thing' is very true. For this reason, I do not intend to go into any detail regarding specific techniques – these are best learned on a course. However, particularly in a mountain environment, it is of the utmost importance that you realize that you are performing *first* aid, the sole function of which is to comfort victims and keep them alive until such time as a specialist can take over. Unless you know exactly what you are doing, it is better to leave such things as fractures to the experts, and concentrate on the essentials.

Immediate action will be required if the victim is not breathing, has no pulse or heartbeat, or is bleeding severely. If any of these three conditions are left untreated, they will result in rapid death. Therefore, as an absolute minimum, you should know how to perform mouth-to-mouth (or mouth-to-nose) respiration, cardiac compression, and how to stop severe bleeding. You should also recognize the dangers of injuries to the head, neck, chest, and spine, and know how to place a casualty in the coma position.

It is worth noting that many people are horrified by the amount of blood which flows during most mountain accidents. Consequently, because the volume is generally unexpected, many first aid kits contain insufficient absorbent material to deal with it. Try not to be overwhelmed by the sight of so much blood, and remember that a person can lose a pint or so without too much ill effect. A pint of blood will appear to be an incredible amount.

No matter how mild the injuries, you should always treat the victim for shock. If he is conscious, reassurance is one of the best medicines available. Do not underestimate the value of morale; you can worry all you like, but you must never show the victim that you are worried. For similar reasons you should try to keep calm; panic can be a killer.

Accident victims are highly susceptible to mountain hypothermia (See section 3.2) and frost-bite (See section 3.4). Assuming you can stabilize their condition, you should do everything in your power to protect them from further harm from these conditions. If the casualty is conscious and there is no risk of spinal injury, you may be able to move him to a more sheltered position. If, on the other hand, he is unconscious, or if you suspect spinal damage, you should try to build the shelter around him. Such casualties should not be moved unless their life is threatened by stonefall (See section 4.5), avalanche (See section 4.4), or some other uncontrollable hazard.

FIRST AID KIT

Artificial resuscitation can usually be done without any extra equipment. Severe bleeding can be stopped without bandages. However, in order to increase both the chances of survival and the comfort of any casualty, you will require some basic items and a simple first aid kit should therefore be regarded as an essential. Generally speaking, you will find it better to make your own than to buy a ready-made one. Apart from the fact that it will probably be cheaper, you can make sure that it contains only those items which you feel you will need. If individual items can be used for more than one purpose, so much the better.

The more important items include two or more triangular bandages, medium and large wound dressings, a 4 inch elasticated bandage, a selection of adhesive dressings (band-aids), and a roll of one inch zinc oxide plaster. A pair of round-nosed scissors will be useful for cutting bandages and dressings, and a small pack of analgesics such as paracetamol or aspirin will not go amiss. It is also sound practice to carry a waxed luggage label and a chinagraph pencil so that you can write down the details of any accident (See section 1.7).

There are various items which are applicable more to one season than another, for example, salt tablets, sunscreen, and insect repellent. Other common items include moleskin, micropore and artificial skin (for blisters), calamine cream (for burns), indigestion tablets, etc. Do not forget to take sufficient quantities of any personal medicines, and if you suffer from a condition which requires regular medication, it is a good idea to carry the details in writing.

I cannot overemphasize the importance of attending a good, practical first aid course; this will be time and money well spent. After all, whether you are in the mountains or at home, the principles remain the same, and you never know when you might need them.

Part four

Mountain conditions

4.1 Introduction

We have looked at basic mountain safety, at the ways in which
mountains alter the weather, and at a number of ailments which can
affect us when we are on the hill. In this final part of the book we
are going to be concerned not so much with the effects of the
mountains as with the mountains themselves.

Every upland area is unique. Not only do different ranges form
different landscapes, but they also have their own special
atmosphere. Whilst these atmospheres are purely psychological,
there are usually enough physical differences to present the visitor
with a particular set of difficulties which will not be met in the same
combination elsewhere. Taken singly, each problem may be the
same wherever you go; the hazards arise from their unique
combination.

We have seen that psychology plays an important part in the
avoidance of certain human conditions; the same applies to the
various mountain conditions. Some areas feel dangerous, they have
a brooding atmosphere and we take more care because of it. In
other areas, the atmosphere feels friendly and although we may
think we are alert to potential hazards, it is all too easy to become
blasé.

Landscape plays an important role in the atmosphere of an area,
and can therefore affect our attitudes. The very shape of the hills
can alter our mood and cause us to take more or less care. Rough
and rugged areas like the Rhinogs, or the limestone moors to the
west of the Carmarthen Fan, can present such difficult ground
conditions that they demand a high degree of concentration;
because of this, one tends to treat them with respect. The same
applies to particularly rocky or craggy regions such as the Black
Cuillins of Skye. Conversely, gentle, rounded hills like the Brecon
Beacons or the Black Mountains appear to demand far less
concentration, but if you have ever been caught in unexpectedly

bad weather in such areas, you will know how difficult life can become. As well as a distinct lack of shelter (See section 3.5), the featureless nature of the terrain can cause problems with navigation.

The combination of landscape and weather often affects our mood. The best illustration is a situation known to most rock climbers: the friendly cliff which you visited on a sunny day seems a totally different place when the cloud is down and everywhere is damp and gloomy. The effect can be so marked as to turn the fun climb of a previous visit into a fairly serious epic. Not only do the mountains have an effect on the weather, but the weather also has an effect on the mountains.

In the following section we will look at the variety of ground conditions which can be found in the mountains. Different types of terrain will cause different potential hazards which can vary considerably with the weather conditions and the time of year. For example, even when there is no snow around, different forms of ice can present major hazards.

Mountains being mountains, the terrain rarely stays flat, and as the ground climbs towards the vertical, other factors come into play. In winter conditions both cornices and avalanches present a far more common hazard than many people think. In summer loose rock and stonefall can be potential hazards, and although it will mainly affect those of you who go rock climbing or scrambling, if your walking route takes you anywhere near the base of a cliff or a long slope (particularly one formed from, or containing, scree), you should be aware of the risks.

No matter what the time of year, any movement on steep ground requires care, concentration, and a certain amount of technique. The fact that so many mountain accidents involve falls suggests that people either underestimate the dangers or overestimate their own abilities. You are as likely to injure yourself during a tumbling fall down a grassy slope, as you are by falling over the edge of a small but vertical outcrop. In fact, because most people will take more care at the top of the outcrop, it is arguable that the grassy slope is the more dangerous of the two.

Crossing mountain streams in another major hazard often

underestimated. Such streams usually contain surprisingly cold
water flowing very swiftly over a bed composed of rocks and
boulders which are frequently loose and slippery.

Although many of these hazards are uncontrollable, simple
awareness will enable you to calculate the risks involved. Whether
the risks can be justified is something only you can decide.

4.2 Ground conditions

No two mountains are ever the same. Apart from differences in
shape and size (which generally only change very slowly), they vary
widely in the texture of their surface. Whilst many of these textures
are permanent, formed as a result of the geological history of the
area, others are more transitory, especially those caused by
seasonal vegetation, climatic effects, and the works of man. In this
section we are concerned with these textures – with the many
different types of terrain you can expect to meet when on the hill.

PATHS

To begin with, your visits into the mountains will almost certainly
be centred upon reasonably well-defined paths. The best of these
can be a joy to follow, being the result of decades (if not centuries)
of use. In addition to following a natural route through their
surroundings, they invariably make the best use of local features,
taking the easiest line when climbing or descending steep slopes,
and avoiding both visible and unseen obstacles. Conservation of
energy is one of the prime requirements of good mountaincraft,
therefore it is better to stay on the path than to try and take short
cuts. Apart from the extra energy used in crossing rough ground,
taking short cuts is the best way to discover that the shortest
distance between two points is seldom the easiest or the quickest.

When on these paths in a group, try not to crowd each other.
There is nothing as annoying as someone trying to walk by your side
on a single-track path, or having your heels trodden on because the

Paths come in many different shapes, surfaces and widths. This picture shows part of
the Pyg Track in Snowdonia.

person behind you is too close. Similarly, if you need to retie a
bootlace or wish to stop to take a photograph, do so where you will
not impede the progress of others. You are not going to be very
popular with the person immediately behind you if you suddenly
stop in the middle of the path for no apparent reason.

It is a sad fact of life that good paths are becoming increasingly
rare. The intensive use of the more popular routes has led, in
places, to devastating erosion, often resulting in awkward surfaces
and unsightly scars. Indeed, many of the classic paths are now so
badly worn that some sections are difficult to follow, and although
there are a few notable exceptions, a large proportion of the
attempts to combat the problem have simply made matters worse.
Although the whys and wherefores of path improvement do not
concern us here, both badly-eroded and badly-repaired paths can
present potential hazards, especially if they have a deeply rutted or
loose surface. If you are forced to follow such routes, make sure
that you place your feet carefully, with the entire sole on the
ground.

When faced with such problems, many people walk beside the
path. Although certain authorities will beg, bully and even order
you not to do this (the logic being that yours and several hundred
other pairs of boots will quickly widen the scar), there is sometimes
very little alternative. If you do forsake the path because the mud
has become thigh deep, or because a sudden downpour has turned it
into something resembling a white-water canoe course, try to walk
as far to one side as practicable.

Once you have been into the hills a few times, you will probably
start to find path erosion very depressing, and it will not be long
before you feel the need to strike out for the open fell. It is at this
stage that you will discover the problems associated with different
types of terrain.

SHORT GRASS
Despite the fact that the epitome of a mountain is a rocky peak, you
will often find yourself walking on vegetation, notably grass,
heather, and bilberry. Of these, short grass (usually sheep cropped)
is undoubtedly the most pleasant, although it can be surprisingly

slippery when either very wet or very dry. This is particularly true if you are wearing rock boots, and climbers should bear this in mind when descending from mountain cliffs. The only way to reduce the hazard is to place the feet carefully and deliberately, using local lumps and bumps as buffers (See section 4.6).

Care must also be taken when on grass slopes in winter, for even gentle slopes can be lethal when covered with a thin layer of snow or ice. I have had to use crampons to enable safe progress on frozen turf in the Brecon Beacons. Although this is one answer, it is certainly not perfect, and you must exercise extreme caution.

LONG GRASS AND TUSSOCKS

If the grass is long or tussocky, it is a totally different matter. The art of walking in the mountains is to conserve energy and keep a steady, rhythmic pace. If you want to speed up, you increase your length of stride; if you want to slow down, you decrease it. Long grass drags at your ankles and makes walking surprisingly strenuous. The best way to avoid problems is to walk in an exaggerated, flat-footed stomp. Tussocks, on the other hand, can totally destroy your rhythm. One solution is to decide whether to place your feet on top of them or between them. Personally, unless they are widely spaced, I usually step on top, but many people believe this increases the risk of a broken ankle and so walk between them. Only experience will tell you what is right for you.

HEATHER AND BILBERRY

Heather and bilberry are both common plants in mountain areas, their effects depending upon their state of growth. When low and well spread, they both present few problems, and can be useful when scrambling as they are fairly tough. However, it is bad practice to use vegetation of any kind as a handhold because it is never totally reliable.

If the heather is deep, or the bilberry occurs in large cushions, life can get very miserable. Walking through cushions of bilberry is like walking across a mattress of beach balls filled with sand – sometimes your foot sinks slightly and is cushioned; at other times it hits a hard, rounded object and you are forced to flex your ankle.

Walking through deep heather, on the other hand, is like trying to force your way across a giant brillo pad. Not only do the tough, wiry stems grab at your feet, threatening to trip you up at every move, but also they do a fairly good job of abrading your ankles. The only successful method of avoiding such problems is to find and follow sheep tracks, even though these have a nasty habit of changing direction when you least want them to. In the long run, assuming reasonable visibility, you will probably find it easier and quicker to zig-zag on animal tracks than to force your way straight through.

BRACKEN

Bracken is another plant which grows in profusion on many mountain slopes. If tall and green, it can effectively block your way, making forward progress both difficult and frustrating. In dry weather you will be plagued by insects; in wet weather you will simply get soaked. Even if you keep to paths and animal tracks, bracken can grow fairly high and may overhang the path at between chest and waist height. This means that you often cannot see where you are putting your feet, with obvious hazards. Even when dead, bracken can be slippery, and often manages to find its way into the most unlikely of places.

Although the plant rarely grows on the tops, you may have to walk through a band of it on your way to the open fell. If this happens, try to avoid problems by following the wider paths wherever possible. Never use bracken as a handhold, for not only does it have very shallow roots which can pull out of the ground without warning, but the stems can splinter and give a bare palm a nasty and extraordinarily painful wound.

BOG

Rainfall in mountainous areas tends to be high and drainage poor thus many mountain regions contain large areas of boggy ground. Indeed, many southerners consider places like Kinder Scout and Bleaklow to consist of little else but bog. Despite what you may

Mynydd Llangatwg. When walking across tussocky ground it is often easier to follow sheep tracks.

hear, the bottomless bog is seldom more than an old wives' tale –
there are very few really dangerous bogs in the British mountains.
However, the worst areas should be avoided whenever possible, as
they are not particularly pleasant. Shaking bogs are more alarming
than hazardous. I have only once seen anyone break through the
surface (he was a well-built lad who was jumping up and down to
see what would happen), and he simply disappeared up to mid-thigh
in a foul-smelling ooze. If you find yourself crossing boggy ground,
look for patches of heather and heath as these often indicate drier
areas.

BOULDERS
Boulder fields occur in many mountain areas and can be extremely
awkward to cross. The boulders vary from the size of a golf ball, to
that of a house and whilst the larger ones are usually fairly stable,
the smaller ones may move. Inclined boulder fields are known as
scree slopes or scree.

Take great care when crossing boulder fields as it is all too easy to
break an ankle. Try to resist the temptation to leap from boulder to
boulder – sooner or later you are bound to land on a loose one.
Take care when wending your way between exceptionally large
boulders via narrow clefts, because the ground in between is often
damp and coated with slippery lichen or moss.

Many summits are composed of boulders. When resting at such
places, beware the old tins and broken bottles which ignorant and
inconsiderate people have 'hidden'. I was once admiring the view
from the summit of Tryfan when another visitor leant back on his
arms and seriously cut his wrist on broken glass hidden between two
boulders.

The worst terrain you will ever meet in Britain is boulders
covered by vegetation. Anyone who has visited the Rhinogs will
know exactly what I mean. The vegetation hides cracks and crevices
just wide enough to trap an ankle, and apparently firm footholds
can turn out to be loose rocks at the point of balance. When you are
not perched uncomfortably on small rocks, you are clambering over

Cwm Bychan. Try to follow paths through bracken whenever possible.

larger ones, and even if you take great care, forcing a way through such an area is tiring and frustrating work.

SOLID ROCK
There are few really extensive areas of level solid rock in Britain. However, when it does occur it often forms a reasonable walking surface. One particular bare rock surface that deserves special mention is limestone pavement. Most common in the Pennines (particularly around Ingleborough), these are relatively flat areas of limestone in which the joints have been deeply etched by the chemical action of rain water. Well-eroded pavements can cause problems because it can be difficult to know whether to walk in the grikes (the gaps) or on the clints (the ridges). It is usual to walk along the surface of the relatively wide clints trying to avoid putting a foot into narrow but often deep grikes. Deep pot-holes and fissures can be a hazard in such areas.

INDUSTRIAL REMAINS
Unexpected holes can be a hazard around many old mining areas. These are more common in the mountains than many people think, the copper mines of Coniston and Beddgelert, the lead mines of Plynlumon, and the slate mines of the Moelwyns being good examples. Abandoned quarries can be almost as dangerous, full of loose rock and unstable cliffs. Unless you know what you are doing and have the correct equipment, you would be well advised to keep away from all old industrial relics. Uncapped shafts, in particular, can be extremely dangerous and may be totally hidden beneath vegetation.

EFFECTS OF RAIN
Weather can obviously play a large part in determining or modifying ground conditions. Torrential rain can turn paths and gullies into seething water-courses; drizzle can form a thin but slippery layer of mud over hard-packed, earthy ground, particularly

Descending Pen Cerrig-calch. Crossing terrain composed of boulders can be extremely awkward.

after prolonged dry spells. Even on well-trodden paths, rocks and boulders may be greasy and slippery in moist weather – an important consideration if you are traversing above steep ground. Although there is no magic formula which will enable you to avoid such areas, careful placement of the feet can substantially reduce the risk of slipping (See section 4.6).

SNOW AND ICE

It is when the temperature drops and snow begins to fall that weather will have its most profound effect on the terrain. We have already seen that a thin coating of ice can make gentle grass slopes hazardous, but veneers of ice will obviously cause problems wherever they occur (See section 2.3). Some of the hazards may be reduced by wearing crampons (See section 4.6), but there are two problems. Firstly, many forms of ice are too thin to provide enough purchase for the crampon teeth; secondly, crampons themselves can be dangerous if used incorrectly.

One of the more difficult surfaces is that caused by a thin layer of loose snow over ice or frozen grass. Many people who wear crampons in these conditions do not realize that the snow can quite easily compact and stick (or ball up) beneath the sole of the boot, the end result being that they wander along feeling more secure, when they are in fact walking on solid blocks of ice. When you wear crampons in snowy conditions, frequently tap the end of your ice axe against your boots as you walk, to try to dislodge the accumulating snow. Alternatively, wrap the frame of the crampons in insulating tape or some form of nylon material; this will reduce the amount of balling quite considerably. You can also tie plastic bags over your boots.

Balling can occur even when you are not wearing crampons. Snow becomes compacted in the cleats of your boots reducing their traction.

Deep snow is as much of a hazard as thin snow over ice, especially

Cwm Bychan copper mine. Old mine workings can be very hazardous to the unwary. This chasm (known as 'Stopes') is hidden amongst rough ground and is approximately thirty metres deep.

when it is fresh. Anyone who has tried to walk or, more accurately, wade through even a small drift will appreciate the problems. The deeper the snow, the more energy you will need to force a passage, and for this reason it is best to follow in the footsteps of the trail-breaker, a role which should be frequently swopped if the deep snow continues for any length of time. Wherever there are large accumulations of fresh snow on mountain slopes, there will be a risk of avalanche (See section 4.4).

Thinly crusted snow can be frustrating, painful and exhausting, especially if the crust periodically breaks under your weight. Apart from destroying your rhythm, you will sink forward against the sharp crust every time you break through, which can cause severe bruising if continued for any length of time. There is no foolproof method of avoidance, although walking with a shuffling, sliding gait, trying to avoid pushing the foot hard on the crust, can sometimes help.

Snow of this type can be extremely hazardous during steep descents, for you can seriously injure your knees if you break through when moving fast. If you are forced to descend such slopes, move slowly and cautiously, stamping your feet in order to break through the crust.

Even when the crust refuses to take any weight your rhythm will be destroyed, for there is a momentary pause before the crust breaks. In this time you have usually put a fair amount of weight on your foot, then, when the break occurs, your foot drops suddenly, jerking you forward. If you are unable to force your way through the snow like a plough, the only way of reducing the inconvenience is to step heavily and break the crust with as much force as possible. This, too, is tiring.

Solid snow usually provides an excellent surface on which to walk. However, on sloping surfaces it can be extremely dangerous for it can be difficult to stop a trip turning into a slide. If the slope steepens, ends in rocks, or leads towards the edge of a precipice, such a slide could be fatal. Methods of avoiding such hazards will be

Winter walking in Snowdonia. An ice axe should be regarded as an essential piece of equipment in such conditions.

discussed in section 4.6.

In addition to forming deep drifts, the wind can blow the snow over potential hazards, hiding them from view. It is quite possible for snow to cover the ice of a mountain lake, with obvious dangers for anyone unfortunate enough to cross unwittingly. Windblown snow can also form bridges across streams, and may even hide fissures and cracks in boulder fields and limestone pavements. Generally speaking, pothole entrances will remain relatively clear of snow because the warmer air which usually rises out of them in cold weather will melt any snow cover. The same is often (although not always) true of old mine shafts. Short of staying at home, there is little that anyone can do to remove completely the risks posed by such hidden hazards, although some, like lakes and large streams, can be avoided through good map interpretation and navigation.

EFFECTS OF THAW

Changes in temperature can have a marked effect on winter terrain. They can cause cornices to collapse (See section 4.3), avalanches to start (See section 4.4), and may even be responsible for stonefall (See section 4.5). On a daily basis, the firm snow of the morning may be wet and porridgey by the afternoon because of diurnal temperature variations. Although this is especially important when visiting the Alps (and explains the reasons for early Alpine starts), it can also make a marked difference to conditions in Britain. Winter days should be planned accordingly.

A sudden thaw after a prolonged cold spell can sometimes cause a layer of surface mud to form over ground which is still frozen, especially if the thaw is accompanied by rain. Such surfaces should be avoided if they are sloping.

4.3 Cornices

A cornice is an overhanging mass of snow, formed at the top of certain slopes by the action of the wind. Alpine cornices can be gigantic, and although those found in Britain are small in comparison, they can still present a major threat, especially in the Scottish Highlands. The mechanisms by which they are formed are

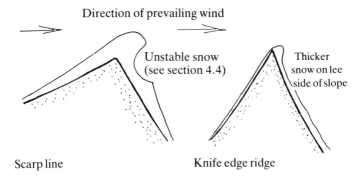

Fig. 34. Cornice formation

fairly complex, but luckily you do not need a degree in snow mechanics to appreciate their inherent hazards.

PROBABLE SITES
Cornices form at the junction of two slopes, and always face away from the wind which builds them. You will probably find it fairly useful to think of them as an unstable extension of the windward slope. If this slope is long and smooth, the cornice will be correspondingly large. Conversely, if the slope is short or steep, the cornice will be small (Fig. 34). In practical terms, this means that you are more likely to find a cornice at the edge of a plateau than on a knife-edge ridge. Contrary to popular belief, it is the angle of the windward slope which is critical, for this acts as a reservoir of snow which can be easily moved towards the edge.

There are three situations where cornices may present a hazard: they may collapse as you walk above them, they may collapse as you walk below them, and they can form a dangerous barrier at the top of otherwise easy snow gullies and winter climbs.

APPROACH FROM ABOVE
When approaching a cornice from the windward side, it may be extremely difficult, if not impossible, to see. The danger is that you

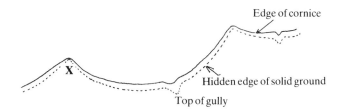

Fig. 35. Viewing cornice hazard on curving scarp (plan view). By standing at X one can view the scarp edge to see how large are the cornices

will step onto the unsupported part of the structure and either fall straight through, or cause it to collapse. Great care must therefore be taken when approaching steep slopes from a windward direction in snowy conditions, especially if you are looking for the start of a descent route and therefore need to go fairly close to the edge.

Sometimes it may be possible to gain a vantage point from where you can look to see if there are any cornices, particularly when the scarp curves (Fig. 35). At other times, fracture lines or partial slumps may be visible, and these should be taken as a warning. Remember, when a cornice collapses, it often takes a sizeable chunk out of the slope behind it, so the line of collapse is generally far further back than most people realize (Fig. 36).   One hazard which often goes unrecognized concerns boulders or patches of bare rock which can be seen at intervals through the snow. These are often taken as an indication of solid ground below, and people tend to walk straight from the one to the other, thinking that they will be on solid ground, possibly keeping to one side to avoid potential fracture lines. Whilst this is generally a perfectly acceptable technique, there are times when the edge of the scarp may curve into bays between headlands. if this is the case, your route could take you inside the fracture line (Fig. 37).

Avoiding such hazards is simply an extension of recognizing that they exist. It is safest to work on the assumption that the potential fracture line is always far further back than you have calculated. If

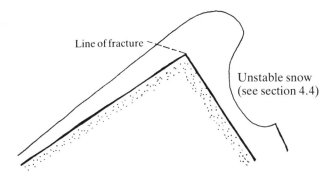

Fig. 36. Cornice fracture line

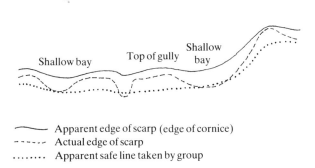

—— Apparent edge of scarp (edge of cornice)
- - - - - Actual edge of scarp
. . . . Apparent safe line taken by group

Fig. 37. Cornice hazard over gullies and bays. By referring to
Fig. 36, which shows that the fracture line is further back than is
normally supposed, you will appreciate that the route shown here
is potentially very hazardous

you are looking for the start of a descent route, or need to approach the edge for any other reason, it makes sense to have a safety line (See section 4.6), especially if you are unsure of the ground.

APPROACH FROM BELOW

When approaching a cornice from below, there are a number of factors which should be considered. The very presence of a cornice indicates potential avalanche conditions, for there will invariably be an accumulation of snow on the lee slopes directly below (See section 4.4). Even if this is relatively stable, the strength of the cornice may be questionable, but this will be extremely difficult to predict without physical examination. It is not a very good idea to examine an unstable cornice from below!

You may get some indication of conditions by looking at neighbouring slopes, for if cornices have recently collapsed nearby, it is fairly safe to assume that all those in the area are suspect. However, do not make the mistake of thinking that this works the other way around; just because no cornices have collapsed does not mean that they are all stable.

Cornices are most likely to collapse during a thaw, in or immediately after a snowstorm, or when there have recently been winds strong enough to drift the local snow. These are also classic avalanche conditions, and even if an avalanche does not occur of its own right, the collapse of a cornice will almost certainly precipitate one (See section 4.4). Collapsing cornices can therefore constitute a fairly serious hazard to people walking along the base of the slope which they overhang.

Cornices can also constitute a major hazard during winter climbing because they form a final, possibly unstable barrier which guards the end of the climb. Although there may sometimes be an easy way to avoid this, it is often necessary to remove some of the snow. This is usually done either by cutting a slot or, if the cornice is large, by tunnelling up through the snow. It is important to take

It is often necessary to cut a slot in a cornice in order to finish a winter climb. If the cornice is exceptionally large, you may even have to tunnel through.

such problems into consideration when planning your start, for breaking through a cornice will not only take a long time, but will also be extremely strenuous, especially when undertaken by climbers who are already tired after a long day. Under these conditions, benightment is an ever present hazard. The greatest danger, however, is that if the cornice is already weak (perhaps because of a slow rise in the temperature throughout the day), such cutting and tunnelling may further weaken it to the extent that it could collapse. For this reason you should always try to arrange a good belay (See section 4.7) well to one side of the place where you intend to attack the snow. It also makes sense to start (and finish) winter climbing as early as possible.

4.4 Avalanche

Avalanches represent a far more common hazard in the British mountains than many people realize. Although they are most likely to occur in the Scottish Highlands, they can occur in any area – given sufficient snow, there could even be avalanches on the South Downs.

A detailed discussion of the causes of effects of avalanches would require a book in itself, and there is only space here to skim the surface of what is an extremely complex subject. You do not need to know all the technicalities in order to appreciate the hazards, but a basic understanding of the mechanisms involved is essential, especially if you intend to visit such areas as the Cairngorms and the North-West Highlands in winter. As with all forms of mountaincraft, knowledge of the theory is not enough, you must get experience of the various types of snow before you are able to judge conditions with any sort of accuracy.

SNOWFLAKES

Different atmospheric conditions produce different types of snowflakes. The various flakes include needles, plates, capped columns, and spatial dendrites. Their occurrence is affected by ground and air temperatures, lapse rate, humidity, windspeed, and turbulence. The same combination of conditions rarely occurs, thus in two successive snowfalls, the layer of flakes deposited in each fall will be slightly different.

METAMORPHISM

It is important to realize that snowflakes are unstable and will change their shape over a period of time. This change is known as metamorphism, and starts as soon as the flake is formed in the atmosphere. A good example is that warm temperatures can cause small snow crystals to clump together to form large, sticky flakes.

Although certain types of snowflake are more prone to avalanche than others, it is the changes which occur after the snow has fallen in which we are most interested. In Britain, this is usually destructive metamorphism, so called because the original crystal structure of the flake is changed. In practical terms, individual crystals become simplified and freeze together, forming a strong bond. This results in the snow layer settling and becoming more stable, thereby reducing the risk of certain types of avalanche.

When the temperature hovers around 0°C, freeze-melt metamorphism can occur. This results in the formation of larger crystals within some of the snow layers and can lead to marked differences in stability. Different layers of snow with different characteristics, are often separated by definite junctions. During the day, when the temperature may rise above freezing, meltwater percolates downward until it meets an impermeable layer, at which point it flows along the junction forming a lubricant along which the upper layers may slide. If it reaches the ground, it may even melt or wash away a thin band of consolidated snow leaving the remaining layers effectively unsupported.

Constructive metamorphism can occur if temperatures remain well below freezing point for any length of time. Under these circumstances, the surface layers can be far colder than those close to the ground, and water vapour will rise through the layers and may recrystallize, the process resulting in large unbonded crystals of depth hoar or sugar snow. These will form a weak layer which, in addition to acting as a lubricant, may suddenly fail and cause an avalanche. Conditions severe enough to cause this type of metamorphism are rare in Britain, although depth hoar is occasionally found in Scotland.

The final type of metamorphism occurs during a thaw, when the temperature rises so quickly that the crystalline structure is destroyed before the snow has a chance to melt. This will result in a loss of cohesion which will cause the snow to flow down the nearest slope.

OTHER FACTORS

In addition to the various types of metamorphism, a number of other factors are relevant in the formation of avalanche conditions. Avalanches can only occur if there is sufficient snow, and generally speaking, the greater the amount of snow that falls, the more likely it is to avalanche before it has a chance to settle. Eighty per cent of all avalanches occur during or immediately after heavy snowfalls.

Avalanches, obviously, will not descend unless there is a slope down which they can travel. To a certain extent, the steeper the slope, the more likely it is to avalanche, but there comes a point beyond which the angle is so great that snow cannot accumulate in sufficient quantities and so the risk decreases. Surprising as it may seem, the most dangerous slopes are those at a medium angle of between 30° and 45°, but avalanches can occur on any slope, and should be considered a potential risk on slopes of between 20° and 60°.

Whenever snow accumulates on sloping ground it will begin to move slowly downhill under the influence of gravity. Normally it does this very slowly and sedately through plastic deformation, the process at work when the snow on your roof creeps down and overhangs the gutter. Under certain circumstances stresses and strains are set up which cannot be relieved by normal means, and this can result in the layers snapping. When this happens an avalanche may result, especially if freeze-melt or constructive metamorphism have caused poor cohesion between layers or between the snow mass and the ground. Such stresses are often caused by the stretching of the snow layers as they move over convex slopes, and many avalanches start from such points (Fig. 38).

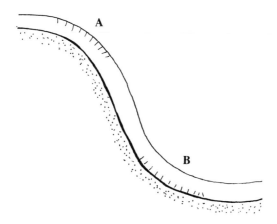

Fig. 38. Stress in snow layers moving over convex slope. The
surface snow layer at point **A** is being stretched so much that the
weight of snow beneath it could cause it to snap. The surface snow
layer at point **B** is being compressed whilst the underlying layers
are being stretched.

WINDSLABS

The importance of the wind is frequently underestimated. It can
cause large masses of snow to accumulate through drifting, even
when there has been no new snowfall. Often found on leeward
slopes, these accumulations are deposited in layers known as
windslabs which can vary greatly in their degree of hardness.
Generally speaking, the higher the windspeed, the harder the slab.
In the same way that constructive and freeze-melt metamorphism
can cause lubricated junctions between different layers of snow,
successive windslabs may be poorly attached to their neighbours
and can therefore present an extremely high risk. Not only are slab
avalanches the most common type in the British mountains, but also
they are extremely difficult to predict.

TYPES OF AVALANCHE

Although it is not intended to go into details, a brief description of the types of avalanche which may occur in Britain will not go amiss. However, classification is a dangerous thing; one type of avalanche may trigger another involving a complex interplay of causes and features.

Slab avalances can occur as two types: soft slab (formed by winds with speeds not exceeding 50 kilometres per hour), and hard slab (formed by wind speeds greater than 50 kilometres per hour). Of the two, the soft slab avalanche is by far the more common, frequently occurring during and immediately after snowfall, particularly when the wind has deposited large quantities of snow on leeward slopes. Movement generally involves only the surface layers which, although usually released as slabs, can pulverize into fine crystals.

Hard slab avalanches usually occur after very cold, very windy weather, and are often associated with constructive metamorphism. They are extremely dangerous because not only is it difficult to diagnose when they are likely to occur, but also their solid surface lulls one into a false sense of security. Like soft slab avalanches, it is generally only the surface layers that are involved; unlike soft slab avalanches, the surface does not disintegrate into crystals but breaks into a number of hard blocks.

The other type of avalanche that regularly occurs in Britain is the wet avalanche. These are caused by thaw conditions and therefore are most common during spring. They also frequently occur when a heavy snowfall starts cold and then gets warmer, eventually turning to rain (See sections 2.5 and 2.7). Although they move relatively slowly, they may start on very shallow slopes (i.e. of less than 20°), and can be extremely destructive, containing large boulders of snow and carrying with them huge amounts of debris. A major problem is that they freeze solid as soon as they stop.

Although not common in Britain, powder avalanches do occur, although many are really slab avalanches in which the slab has been

Crib Goch in winter. Even south of the Scottish border one should be wary of avalanche conditions.

pulverized. They travel extremely quickly (speeds in excess of 45 metres per second have been recorded) and are normally accompanied by an intense shock wave. True powder avalanches usually affect north and east facing slopes during extremely cold dry weather, or if there are sudden heavy snowfalls after a cold spell or on to a solid crust. The most common cause of death in such avalanches is suffocation.

Finally the climax avalanche, rare even in Scotland, is caused by the sudden failure of one or more layers. Such failures are usually due to weaknesses caused by constructive metamorphism, and will not occur until after a prolonged spell of very cold weather. They are usually primed by fresh snowfall, and can reach devastating proportions as they often involve the whole depth of snow.

AVOIDANCE

It is an unfortunate but telling fact that the vast majority of avalanches are caused by their victims. If you are unsure about the risk, *ask the locals*. In addition to knowing what the past weather has been like, they will also know of any local peculiarities. Smooth slabs and grassy slopes do not make good foundations for snow and avalanches may occur frequently from these areas, the slabs below Coire an Lochan being a good example.

We have already stated that the majority of avalanches occur during or shortly after storms. This is because the fresh snow has not had a chance to settle. The time it takes to become stable will depend very much upon the temperature. Although the high risk period usually only lasts for about forty-eight hours, it may be far longer, particularly if it is very cold. You should also be wary of any sudden changes in the temperature, especially moving to warmer conditions.

If you think there may be a danger, it is better to keep to the ridges and high ground, avoiding both convex slopes and those between 30° and 45° wherever possible. Leeward slopes are particularly prone to avalanche, and the wind may have caused accumulations of snow even though there has been no recent snowfall. Try especially in warm conditions to keep out of gullies and enclosed valleys, where avalanche debris would bury you, and avoid slopes capped by cornices.

When on the mountain, be aware of the causes of the different types of avalanche, and be alert for any tell tale signs. Listen for hollow booming sounds which might indicate the presence of hard slab; watch for slides of soft slab when you move your feet; look out for cracks or other signs of instability such as subsidence, melting, or rolling snowballs. The best warning of avalanche conditions is recent avalanche activity.

SNOWPITS

You may like to consider digging a small snowpit in order to see the different layers of snow. Although you will be unable to assess the snow profile with any accuracy without special equipment, snowpits can be an extremely useful way of discovering the state of the layers. Any sudden change from a hard layer to a soft one will indicate a risk of avalanche.

CROSSING SUSPECT SLOPES

If you are forced to cross a suspect slope, do so one at a time and do not make the mistake of thinking that because one person has crossed it is safe: crossing may well have weakened the snow sufficiently for the second person to cause an avalanche. Undo the waist strap and loosen the shoulder straps on your rucksack, take off any ice axe loop, and zip up your anorak so that it protects your face (over eighty per cent of avalanche deaths are caused by suffocation). Cross the slope slowly but steadily, working slightly downhill but taking the shortest route available between two stable points (i.e. rocks, trees, etc).

If an avalanche does occur, it is vitally important that other members of the group track the victim for as long as possible, for the longer he stays buried the less likely he is to survive.

AVALANCHE CORDS AND BEACONS

If you take all the necessary precautions, the risk from avalanche will be minimized. It will not, however, be totally negated, and so it is wise for you to carry either an avalanche cord or, better still, an avalanche beacon.

Avalanche cords are long lengths of brightly-coloured nylon cord; one end is tied around your waist, the rest trails along behind you. In the event of being overwhelmed by an avalanche, some part of the cord may be left on the surface, and rescuers can find you by following it. Most good avalanche cords have arrows pointing towards your body at regular intervals along their length.

Avalanche beacons transmit a radio signal which can be picked up by other, similar beacons. Although they are expensive, they may save a life – perhaps even yours. Make sure you are using a beacon with the same frequency as those of your friends.

Under normal conditions, each beacon is switched to the transmit mode, and is worn as recommended (*not* carried in a rucksack). If someone is overwhelmed by an avalanche (at which time they may lose their rucksack), the remaining members of the party switch their beacons to receive mode and proceed to search for the victim. With most types an increase in strength of signal indicates a decrease in distance from the body.

If you and the other members of your party carry such beacons, always check them both in transmit and receive modes before you set out, then leave them in transmit mode for the rest of the day. You may well wish to carry spare batteries.

ACTION IF AVALANCHED

There is very little you can do if you are caught in an avalanche. However, you must try. Your actions will largely depend upon the type of avalanche, but the first thing to do is to work out your best line of escape. Unless you are on the very edge (when it may be possible to outrun it), it is almost always best stay where you are for as long as possible. Driving your ice axe as deep as possible into what might be more stable layers below may help, the logic being that the longer you stay put, the less material there will be to bury you if you do become inundated.

Try to keep your head up, and your back towards the avalanche, and if you start to move, let go of your ice axe, jettison your rucksack, and roll or make backstroke movements towards the side of the slide. Keep your mouth closed and, if possible, cover both your mouth and nose with your anorak hood, balaclava, sweater – anything.

The critical time is as the avalanche slows. If you are still conscious you must make yourself an air space as near to the surface as possible. Flail your arms around, kick, roll, do anything you can to create space around you; remember that the air you now trap may well have to last you until someone finds you and digs you out. Claw your way towards any light that you can see; although you may be totally disorientated, you must get as near the surface as possible, for the deeper you are buried, the less likely you are to survive. You must do these things quickly, before the avalanche stops, because the snow may well set solid within a few seconds of stopping.

AVALANCHE RESCUE

If you witness an avalanche in which people are involved, try to work out where the slide will have taken them. Mark both the position at which they were last seen and the position at which they were first caught, for this may give an indication of where they are buried. Even though you may not be able to do much by yourselves, you must at least make a thorough surface search, digging in any likely positions. If there are enough of you, this can be done while others are summoning help. (See section 1.7). Speed is of the essence.

For those of you that are interested, further details about the cycle of snow, the causes and types of avalanches, avalanche search and rescue, etc, will be found in some of the books listed in Appendix II.

4.5 **Stonefall**

Stonefall is not a major hazard in the British mountains, but accidents caused by falling rocks and stones occur every year with almost monotonous regularity. As with most other accidents, many of them are avoidable.

The most common cause of stonefall is freeze-thaw action (See section 2.3). Particularly in spring, when freeze-thaw is at its height, stonefall can be a common hazard below certain cliffs. Additionally at this time of year, rocks which have been held in place throughout the winter by a permanent covering of snow or ice are suddenly set free, and this may result in even more activity. The loose rocks so formed either remain on ledges until dislodged (usually by climbers or sheep), or fall down the cliff and pile up at the bottom, eventually forming sizeable slopes of loose rock known as scree.

Some scree slopes are dead. These rarely have any rock added to them and have begun to be colonized by plants. Other scree slopes are active and are still growing, being added to every year. Active scree can be recognized by its relative lack of vegetation and the profusion of loose rocks, many of which will be the same size.

An active scree obviously indicates that the cliff above throws down the odd rock or two every now and then. The most hazardous time to walk below these cliffs is after a very cold night, just after the sun has reached the cliff and is beginning to melt any ice.

EVASIVE ACTION

The first sign of danger may be a rattling sound above or, if the cliff is particularly large, the falling stone may be moving so fast that it whistles. The golden rule in this situation is to hug the cliff, hunch your shoulders, and (unless you are wearing a climbing helmet) cover your head with your arms. Admittedly the stone may break your arms, but better a broken arm than a fractured skull. Do not look up to see where the sound is coming from. Nor should you tuck your chin into your chest because this simply leaves a vulnerable area at the base of the neck.

Do not be lulled into a false sense of security by the thought that stonefall only happens on major cliffs. A rock does not have to be very big or fall very far to do a fair amount of damage to the human frame, especially if it hits you on the head. The hazard can therefore be present on any sized cliff, and even grassy slopes with boulders at the top can be dangerous.

The Llangattock escarpment. Even in areas not usually associated with 'rugged' terrain you can often find scree below steep cliffs.

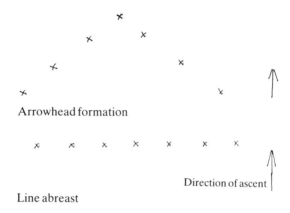

Arrowhead formation

Direction of ascent

Line abreast

Fig. 39. Formations used when ascending scree and slopes containing loose boulders

SCREE
Scree slopes can present a hazard, for it is easy to dislodge rocks onto people below. If you are with a group which is following a route which climbs or descends scree, make sure that you do so either in an arrowhead formation or in a line abreast (Fig. 39). This will reduce the danger of people being hit by falling rocks. Even when traversing scree, take great care not to dislodge rocks for there may be people hidden below you.

GULLIES
Climbing or descending gullies can be extremely hazardous for similar reasons. Gullies tend to be a natural path for stonefall, and often contain much loose rock. Great care should be taken at all times, but particularly during the thaw phase of freeze-thaw action. Once trapped in a gully, a moving rock is going to bounce all over the place, and dodging it will be pure luck. If you are with a group which is moving in a gully, concentrate on where you are putting your hands and feet, and make sure you keep close together. In this way any dislodged rock will not have time to pick up speed. If the

danger seems particularly great, it is wise to let only one person move at a time, while the others stay in some form of shelter.

WARNING SHOUT

If you do dislodge a stone, wherever you are on the hill, make sure you bellow, 'Below!' at the top of your voice, even if you cannot see anyone further down the slope. However, the shout itself does not make the falling stone any softer. Take great care whenever people may be below you and in the line of fire of any stone you move. If you are not a rock climber, spare a thought for those who are whenever you walk near the top of a cliff, especially when there are loose rocks lying around.

MOUNTAINEERING ROUTES

When rock climbing on the larger mountain cliffs such as Lliwedd, you should consider wearing a helmet. On such cliffs there are always loose stones lying around on ledges, and many of the larger cliffs have major paths running along their crests. It is all too easy for rocks to be dislodged from above either by natural means, sheep, parties of walkers or even by fellow climbers.

TRUNDLING

Although the temptation to trundle is often almost overwhelming, please think carefully about the possible results of your actions before you push. A friend of mine once rounded a spur to be faced with a very large, very fast-moving lump of rock which had been deliberately rolled down from above. Had it not been for a much larger boulder behind which he fell (and over which the trundled boulder flew), he would undoubtedly have been killed.

On two separate occasions I have been pelted with stones by ignorant walkers who were casually lobbing blocks down the east face of Tryfan.

THUNDER

Finally, remember that the likelihood of stonefall is dramatically increased during thunder (See section 2.9).

4.6 Steep ground

To the experienced mountain enthusiast, scrambling up and down rocky ridges or traversing steep slopes is all part of a day in the hills. To the less experienced this aspect of mountain activities can often be unnerving, and many people deliberately avoid sharp ridges and the steeper slopes, simply because they cannot justify the risk they feel is inherent in such situations.

Whilst there is nothing wrong with this attitude *per se*, if you visit the mountains with any regularity you are bound to become fairly intimately involved with steep ground sooner or later. It is possible to gain height remarkably quickly, and there may come a time when you suddenly find yourself in an exposed position. For this reason, the ability to move safely over steep terrain should be regarded as an essential part of mountaincraft.

Safe movement over steep ground relies on a strange mix of confidence, caution, and technique. We have already seen that movement in the mountains involves keeping a rhythmic pace, and that speeding up and slowing down are done by altering the length of stride (See section 4.2), the aim being to move steadily, in as relaxed a manner as possible. Exactly the same applies when crossing steep ground.

ASCENT

As the slope begins to steepen and you begin to climb, you should shorten your stride. Try to resist any temptation to edge your boots; flex your ankles so that you can place the sole of each boot flat on the ground in order to get maximum friction (Fig. 40). You will find it a great help to lock each leg at the knee after you have stepped up.

Above a certain angle, it becomes easier to zig-zag rather than attack a slope head-on. Only experience will tell you this angle, for it will vary from person to person. When you start to zig-zag, try to work out in advance not only where you are going to alter direction, but also where you are going to place each foot. No slope is

When ascending steep ground, keep your body as near upright as possible. Resist the temptation to lean in.

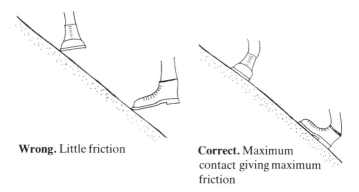

Wrong. Little friction

Correct. Maximum contact giving maximum friction

Fig. 40. Gaining traction on steep ground

perfectly smooth, and you will find life much easier if you use the various lumps and bumps to get more support for the feet, altering direction at the larger ones.

A common mistake is to lean into the slope. Not only can this affect your sense of balance, it will also alter your centre of gravity so that you put an outward pressure on your feet. Although it may feel a little less secure to begin with, you will be far safer if you stand upright (Fig. 41). Generally speaking, it is safer to lean outwards than inwards.

On very steep ground it is better to use your hands to push yourself away from the slope than to succumb to the temptation of grabbing a handhold and leaning into it. The most common result of the latter course of action is that your feet fly away from under you.

DESCENT

When descending steep slopes, exactly the same principles apply. Shorten your stride, keep a rhythmic pace, flex your ankles, and place your feet flat on the ground, making use of any local irregularities of slope. Descending long slopes can put a huge strain on your knees, but if you bend your legs, your thigh and calf muscles will act as shock absorbers, and you will be less likely to

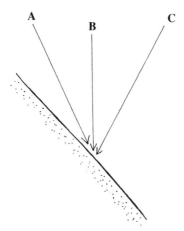

Fig. 41. Position when traversing or zig-zagging.
   A. **Wrong.** Resulting forces push feet away from holds
   B. **Good.** Body weight lying directly over feet
   C. **Good,** but be careful not to overbalance

damage your cartilage. The steeper the angle of descent, the slower
you should go.
   Once again, resist the temptation to lean into the slope, – you
must try to keep upright. If your feet slide out from under you when
you descend, you are probably leaning backwards without realizing
it. In this instance, however, it is better lean backwards than to
make the mistake of over-compensating and leaning so far forwards
that you end up somersaulting down the mountain.

DESCENDING ROCKY GROUND
The descent of steep, rocky slopes is particularly hazardous for it is
often difficult to judge depths, especially in gloomy or misty
conditions, or at dusk. Try to avoid such descents wherever
possible, but if you are forced to use such a slope, always climb
down slowly and carefully. Unless you wish to become cragfast, it is

best not to descend any sections which you cannot reclimb – you may find your path blocked further down.

SCREE RUNNING

It is important that you move slowly and carefully on slopes where there are loose boulders, for any loss of balance could send loose rocks down on your companions or might result in a nasty fall. Generally speaking, the shorter your step, the better.

When descending scree slopes (See section 4.5) in which the rocks are fairly small and uniform, you may find it easier to scree run. Although this can be exhilarating, it is not a technique for the unwary, and should only be used where you can see the whole slope. You must be quite certain that there are no drops or large boulders either on the slope itself or at the bottom, and for this reason it is unwise to run an unknown scree in misty conditions or in bad light because there may be a drop hidden from view (Fig. 42). If

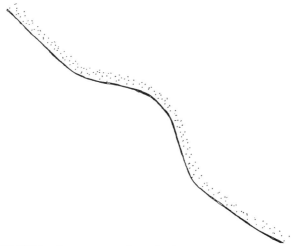

Fig. 42. Hidden drop on scree slope. Such unexpected drops can go un-noticed, especially in gloomy weather. If such a drop were met when scree running it could cause severe problems!

you are in a large party, beware of runaway boulders which may injure those below. In these circumstances it is probably safer to run the scree one at a time than to try and keep close together.

The basic technique is to descend the slope as if you were walking down an escalator, digging your heels well into the stones and keeping your knees slightly bent. You should take short but fairly regular steps. As you start to move down, the stones on which you are standing will begin to slide, and so long as you lean slightly forward, you will slide with them. The combined speed of you walking and the ground moving can be quite fast. Another way of looking at it is that you will always be walking on solid ground, but the solid ground will be moving downwards, quite quickly! When you want to stop, you simply take a little jump and dig both heels well in. As with normal descents, do not lean too far forward, for a somersault in these conditions could lead to serious injury.

Scree running in lightweight boots cannot be recommended – apart from damaging the boots, it could also damage your feet. Additionally, no matter what boots you are wearing, beware of 'classic' scree runs. Most of these have now been used so much that they are becoming dangerously solid.

SCRAMBLING

If the slope becomes so steep that it is necessary to use your hands, you have entered the realm of scrambling, a hazy area lying somewhere between hill walking and rock climbing. By thinking of scrambling as an extension of mountain walking, you will find that many of the techniques of movement on rock tend to fall into place quite naturally. We saw earlier that to move safely up a steep slope you should make use of local irregularities, plan your route in advance, move steadily, and stand upright. The hands, if used at all, were used to push your body away from the slope in order to stay in an upright position. These are exactly the techniques which should be used when scrambling.

The two most common mistakes are over-reliance on handholds, and leaning into the rock. If you remember that you should push up with your feet rather than pull up with your hands, and that you should always be able to look down and see your ankles, you will not go far wrong.

Before you commit yourself to the ascent of a small rock step, work out exactly what route you are going to take. Once done, place your feet deliberately on the holds and climb smoothly and steadily, testing all holds before you put your full weight on them. If you find any loose stones lying on ledges, take great care not to knock them down on to your companions. If you do accidentally dislodge something, shout, 'Below!' immediately. It is no good shouting after the rock has hit the ground.

Remember the old adage about always having three points of contact, and try to keep your heels down and your hands at about shoulder height. Never lunge for a hold – it may not be as good as it looks. If you find that your proposed route is not as easy as you thought, climb back to a safe position and work out a new line.

Scrambling down, although slightly more difficult, is simply a reverse of the above procedures. If you have to descend a rock step, you must make sure that you keep your hands well below shoulder height. Do not be tempted to feel for holds with your feet – look down to see where you are going and place your feet on the holds you can see. Climbing down at night or in poor visibility is extremely dangerous.

Scrambling cannot be taught in a book, nor can the judgement of what is safe and what is stupid. If you intend to do a fair amount of scrambling, you will undoubtedly find it useful to go on a basic rock climbing course. These are offered by many of the organizations listed in Appendix I.

WINTER TECHNIQUES
The techniques used in safe movement on steep ground remain the same no matter what the conditions. However, when there is snow and ice on the hill, there are two other factors which must be taken into consideration. Firstly, movement can sometimes appear to be easier because slopes have been smoothed by snow in which you can

Scrambling – this is NOT the way to do it. The hands are too high, pulling the body so close to the rock that it is impossible to see any holds. Avoid using your knees.

scrape or kick your own irregularities. Secondly, if you do slip, the consequences could be far more serious than in summer, for snow and ice provide very little friction. It is a sad fact that most serious winter accidents are initiated by a simple slip on a gentle slope.

The hazards presented by steep ground in winter should not be underestimated, and you would be well advised to keep away from the steeper slopes of snow and any areas of ice until you have gained a considerable amount of summer experience. Whilst there are some excellent winter walking and mountaineering courses available, a short course of training is no substitute for a long apprenticeship. Even though such courses can show you the techniques better than a book, you will still need to practise and perfect them after the course is over. It is important to keep your enthusiasm in check, even more so in winter.

THE ICE AXE

As noted in section 1.5, you will need a few extra items of equipment if you intend to visit the mountains during the winter months. An ice axe is one of the most important pieces of security equipment you will ever need to buy and, as such, it should not be regarded as an expensive luxury, but an essential. Like other items of modern equipment, ice axes come in a bewildering array of shapes and sizes, many of which are only suitable for technical ice climbing, some of which are little better than walking sticks. An ice axe suitable for general purposes is shown in Fig. 43.

Your ice axe must be of the correct size. For general mountaineering use, the spike should just reach the bottom of the calf when the axe's head is held by your side. If you intend only to walk, the axe can be slightly longer; if you intend to do a fair amount of snow and ice climbing, a shorter axe will be less cumbersome. Although the final choice is yours, it would be wise to visit a good equipment shop before buying, for not only should they be able to show you a range of axes of a suitable length, but also you will have a chance to get the feel of various models. It may sound petty, but it is important that your axe feels right. For these reasons it is unwise to buy an axe via mail order.

There are strong arguments both for and against wrist loops and

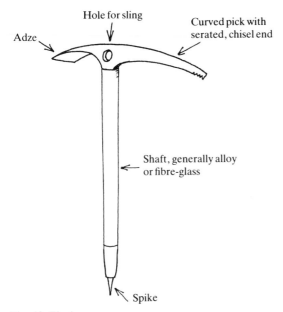

Hole for sling

Adze

Curved pick with
serated, chisel end

Shaft, generally alloy
or fibre-glass

Spike

Fig. 43. The ice axe

slings, some people use them because they reduce the risk of losing
the axe if it is dropped, others do without as they tend to get in
the way. I personally use a sling, but then I also use my axe for
climbing. Once again, although you would be wise to use some form
of attachment to begin with, only experience will show you what is
right for you.

The adze, pick, and spike of your axe should be kept fairly sharp,
and it is advisable to buy head and spike protectors. These should
be used at all times except when the ice axe is being carried in the
hand.

Different people hold their axes in different ways, the standard
position is to hold the head and let the shaft swing down by the leg.
You should find a method which is comfortable, and which does not

present a hazard to fellow travellers. A careless climber once drove the spike of his axe into my shin. Remember to hold the axe in such a way that it is ready for use whenever needed.

ASCENDING SNOW SLOPES

Moving on snow slopes is much the same as moving on any other type of slope, the differences tend to balance each other out. For example, although it is far easier to slip on a snow slope, it is also easier to make your own holds exactly where you want them.

Generally speaking, both when ascending and descending, your ice axe is used as a means of balance and support. This is best achieved by driving the shaft into the snow and holding the head (Fig. 44). The depth to which you drive the shaft will depend upon the steepness of the slope and the hardness of the snow. If the shaft only penetrates a short way, you should reduce the amount of leverage by holding the axe in two hands, the second hand grasping the shaft where it enters the snow (Fig. 45).

In order to secure a solid base for the feet, steps are kicked in the snow by swinging the lower part of the leg from the knee. The harder the snow, the harder the kick. To give maximum support with minimum effort, steps should be large enough to take the front third of the foot, and should slope slightly downwards (Fig. 46). You may have to kick more than once to form a step.

Step kicking is tiring, and can be hard on the feet and boots. You will find it helps to get into some sort of rhythm: two steps, move axe; two steps, move axe . . .

As the slope steepens, you can start to zig-zag in exactly the same way as you would in summer, kicking well in where you intend to change direction. When moving sideways you will find it easier to use the side of your boot to scrape a step (Fig. 47), the disadvantage being that you will not get as much support as when using conventional steps. The ice axe is used in the conventional way, and should be held in the upslope hand. Alternatively, on steeper slopes you may prefer to hold it across the body (Fig. 48). The

Winter mountaineering in the Brecon Beacons. When moving on snow slopes the ice axe should be held in the upslope hand.

Fig. 44. Standard position of ice axe on slope

Fig. 45. Two handed position of ice axe on slope

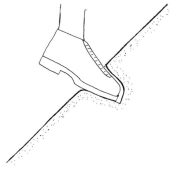

Fig. 46. Kicked step. Sloping slightly down and big enough to take one third of the sole

Fig. 47. Transverse kicked step

Fig. 48. Ice axe position on steeper slopes

disadvantage of the latter method is that it does not give as much support and many people prefer to climb steep snow slopes direct. However, it is important that you know the techniques used in zig-zagging, because they are employed when traversing.

DESCENDING SNOW SLOPES

Descending snow slopes is, in fact, not as difficult as it looks. On steep ground you should face into the slope and kick steps straight down. These will automatically slope inwards because of your position (Fig. 49). Your ice axe should be driven into the snow as far down the slope as practicable. As the angle eases, face away from the slope, leaning forwards and digging your heels well in. *Do not lean back.* It is extremely important that your body weight remains directly over your feet at all times. If you do lean back, your centre of gravity will alter, and you run the risk of sliding out of your holds.

It is not advisable to descend slopes by zig-zagging as it is difficult to get satisfactory support for the feet.

Fig. 49. Step kicking in descent

THE ICE AXE BRAKE

If you use the above techniques, your axe should always be in such a position that you can hold on to it if you lose your footing. However, particularly when traversing and on gentle slopes, there will be times when there is a risk that your axe may come out and that you might start to slide.

Imagine the scene. An axe-less walker is treading his way carefully across gently sloping but hard snow near the top of a minor ridge. Below him the slope steepens slightly before ending in a jumble of large boulders. There are no large cliffs in the immediate area, and the risk of falling on such easy ground seems minimal. The views all around are breathtaking, and because he tries to admire the view and walk at the same time, he stumbles and falls.

Although the ground only slopes gently, the hard snow offers very little friction, and he immediately begins to slide, picking up speed all the time. Trying to dig his hands and feet into the surface has no effect whatsoever, and within a few seconds he is hurtling down the steeper part of the ridge, totally out of control. By the time he reaches the boulders, some twenty seconds later, he will be travelling at well over one hundred kilometres per hour.

Such an accident is avoidable so long as you carry an ice axe and know how to use it. The most important technique is that of the ice axe brake, and it is essential that you learn how to use it both quickly and efficiently in any position. Many people practice ice axe braking by sliding downhill feet first on their stomach, but you are more likely to fall head first, you could easily be on your back, and you may even be somersaulting.

Make no mistake about it – ice axe braking is not an easy technique to master. It requires a great deal of practice before you can use it immediately from any position. The longer you take to apply it, the faster you will be going, and the less likely you are to be able to stop.

The basic idea is to use the pick of the axe as a friction brake. To do this you need to be in a feet-first, face-down position, with one hand over the head of the axe, the adze held into the shoulder, the shaft diagonally across the body, and other hand close to the spike (Fig. 50). Your legs should be kept apart to stop you from rolling, and your feet should be kept clear of the snow until you are almost stationary (particularly important if you are wearing crampons). By tucking in your elbows, you should be able to get a fair amount of weight over the pick, especially if you try to pull up on it. Weight should be applied gently, however, otherwise the pick will bite into

Fig. 50. The ice axe brake

the snow so quickly that the axe will be snatched out of your grip.

If you are not sliding feet first on your front, your first priority is to get into that position. In order to manoeuvre yourself, you should hold the axe firmly with both hands, one hand over the head, the other around the shaft near the pick. When somersaulting, you should stabilize yourself before you do anything else – this is best done by spreading your arms and legs.

If you are falling head first, you should dig the pick into the snow as far as possible to one side of you so that you pivot round into a feet first position.

If you are falling on your back, you should get on to your front by rolling towards the hand holding the head of the axe.

If you are falling head first on your back you have severe problems. The best manoeuvre is to bring the shaft across your stomach, then dig the pick in by your side, swinging yourself under the shaft as you begin to spin. It sounds complicated because it is complicated.

Do not forget that all these actions have to be performed quickly and efficiently as you are bumping with increasing speed down a hard snow slope, possibly heading towards a cliff, and doubtless scared out of your wits.

I cannot over-emphasize the importance of practice, but make sure that you do so on a safe slope. Ideally you need a fairly high, concave slope with a long flat run-out at the bottom. There should be no obstructions of any sort in the area. An acquaintance once broke his leg in three places whilst practising ice axe braking – he hit a fence post.

GLISSADING

If you ever need to descend a slope which is suitable for ice axe brake practice, you can either fall over and practise your braking or you can sit back and slide down the slope, controlling your rate of descent with both the spike of your axe and your heels (Fig. 51). This is known as a sitting glissade, and purists will no doubt hold up their hands in horror at this description, because a true glissade should be done standing up, using the ice axe for support. A standing glissade feels very much like skiing without skis.

Fig. 51. Sitting glissade

Never glissade where you cannot see all of the slope, where there are bumps, boulders, or other obstacles in the way, or if there is any possibility of patches of ice or avalanche.

HARD SNOW AND ICE

Snow can sometimes be so hard that it is impossible to kick steps or even drive the ice axe shaft into the slope. Hard snow and ice present serious hazards which can only be diminished through good judgement and sound technique. For this reason, many books advise you to keep off slopes of hard snow unless you are with an experienced person.

Whilst I agree with these sentiments to a certain extent, anyone who ventures into the mountains in winter is bound to meet hard snow and ice eventually. In any case, because conditions can change with remarkable speed, it is possible that the soft snow you climbed in the morning might have become as hard as ice by the afternoon. It is therefore important that you have a basic knowledge of the techniques which can be used in such conditions.

STEP CUTTING

When the snow becomes so hard that it is impossible to kick steps, you will have to cut them with your ice axe. The most useful (and most common) step of this type is the slash step. As the name suggests, this is cut by slashing the pick across the slope, the resultant groove being long enough and wide enough to take the

Always cut away
from the first step

Fig. 52. Cutting steps

side of the boot. The technique can be extremely useful when
traversing or zig-zagging.

If the situation is such that you require something a little more
substantial than a groove, or if the snow is too soft for the slash step
to hold your weight safely, you will have to cut a larger step. These
are normally cut with the adze (Fig. 52). Be careful not to disturb
the base of the step, and always cut away from the hole formed by
the first chop. You will have to decide whether to attack the slope
direct or in a zig-zag fashion, and how large to cut each step. The
smaller and fewer the steps, the greater the risk of a fall.

Cutting steps down a slope is not an easy task, and it may only be
possible to cut large slash steps. The basic idea is to stand sideways,

Fig. 53. Cutting steps down.
Note the outermost leg is
always the lowest

reach down as far as is safe and cut two holds, one diagonally below the other (Fig. 53). On really steep slopes you will have difficulty in keeping your balance, and may need to hold on to the edge of a higher step. In this case, make sure that the outside leg always remains the lowest, moving it down before the inside leg. Even if you wear a wrist sling, take great care not to drop your axe, for apart from any other considerations, you may instinctively lunge for it, jerking yourself off the holds.

If conditions are particularly icy, you will get more friction from your boots if you wear a pair of woollen socks over them. If you do use this technique, make sure the socks are wool and not nylon, for nylon will decrease the friction rather than increase it.

CRAMPONS
Even when you are an experienced axe swinger, step cutting can be strenuous and time consuming. Nowadays it has to a large extent been replaced by crampon technique, but it is nevertheless an extremely useful skill to have. As we will see, crampons bring with them their own particular hazards, and it is true to say that you can travel safely without them whereas you cannot travel safely without your ice axe.

Crampons can be extremely dangerous pieces of equipment because they can give the wearer a false sense of security. They impart a feeling of invulnerability out of all proportion to the extra safety that they give, and it is very easy to take them for granted and feel that they will give you a secure footing whatever the conditions. Unfortunately, this is not always the case. Not only can snow ball up underneath them (See section 4.2), but they can also slip without warning on verglas or other forms of thin ice, or when moving over the occasional rock step. However, there is no doubt that they can also be very useful when used correctly.

It will not surprise you to learn that there are many different types of crampons available, some suitable only for technical ice climbing, others more suited to wandering around the lower slopes. The fit of the crampons and the way they are attached to the boot is of the utmost importance and, as before, I advise you to visit your local friendly equipment shop. Do not forget to take your boots

Step-in crampons fitted to plastic boots.

with you, for not only will the type of boots be a deciding factor in
the type of crampons you buy, but the crampons will need to be
adjusted to fit them. For this reason is it unwise both to borrow
crampons or to buy them via mail order, unless you know how to
adjust them correctly.

   There are almost as many different types of binding as there are
crampons. Again, advice should be sought from your local

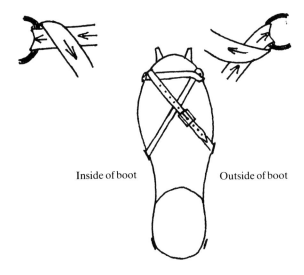

Inside of boot   Outside of boot

Fig. 54. Tying crampon straps

equipment shop. If you buy standard neoprene straps, remember
to tie them the correct way (Fig. 54), otherwise you run the risk of
the toe loop slipping and the crampon working loose. Do not
overtighten the bindings as this could lead to frost-bite (See
section 3.4).

CRAMPON TECHNIQUE
Moving on steep ground with crampons uses the same techniques as
before. However, instead of looking for, kicking, or cutting your
holds, you simply place your feet flat on the slope and walk up. It is
important to flex your ankles and keep your weight directly over
your feet (Fig. 55). Your ice axe is used in exactly the same way as
before.

When the slope steepens further, you either turn sideways to
enable you to point your toes downwards so that your feet lie flat

Fig. 55. Weight distribution when using crampons

against the slope (the French technique), or you face the slope, kick in the front points, and move up (front pointing). This sounds easy, but in practice it is fairly strenuous and requires good technique if the placements are to be at all secure.

The fact that crampon technique seems easy makes it doubly dangerous. Indeed, because front pointing up steep slopes seems so secure, it is even easier to get into exposed positions before you realize what has happened, than in summer. That is when your problems will begin, because front pointing down is much more difficult than front pointing up.

Even on flat, icy ground and gentle slopes, crampons present various hazards. For example, you can often tell if a person uses crampons by the state of their gaiters, because the front points have a habit of snagging the material. It is therefore very easy to trip when wearing crampons, and if you start to slide, they can further complicate matters by catching in the ground and causing you to somersault. They can also cause severe injury. You can avoid tripping by walking with your feet apart, but there is little you can do when you are sliding apart from applying the Ice Axe Brake and trying to keep your feet away from the ground.

In this section it has only been possible to skim the surface of what is one of the most important facets of mountaincraft. Had I written ten times as much, I would still have to state that you cannot learn to move safely on steep ground from a book. This is particularly true of winter conditions, where a simple slip may lead to something far more serious.

For this reason I cannot recommend too highly that you either join a club with experienced members or go on a course. Details of some of the organizations offering suitable courses can be found in Appendix I, and ideas for further reading will be found in Appendix II.

4.7 Ropework

It is a commonly expressed view that only rock climbers should carry ropes into the mountains. There is a certain logic in this, for the very fact that you have a rope may encourage you to cross ground which you would otherwise avoid. Indeed, the rope itself will become a hazard if used incorrectly.

There are also certain arguments in favour of walkers carrying ropes. The most common mention that there have been several walking accidents which could have been prevented had the persons concerned carried a rope and known how to use it effectively. Whilst I do not disagree with this, in the vast majority of cases the situation requiring the rope was the culmination of a series of mistakes. It would be far better to prevent these mistakes occurring in the first place than to try to cure the consequences.

However, it is undoubtedly wise to consider the pros and cons of a rope if you intend to visit rugged, rocky areas, especially if you are the leader of a party of inexperienced people.

It should be noted that the techniques described in this section, although very basic, must be practised *before* they need to be used on the hill. They should only be regarded as emergency measures, for if you go into the mountains intending to use a rope, you should study ropework in far greater detail. Although the procedures will invariably remain the same, there are several ways in which the methods can be improved, most of which require the use of other

Inner Core or 'Kern'

Outer Sheath or 'Mantel'

Fig. 56. Kernmantel climbing rope

knots and other equipment. If you are a rock climber, you will no doubt already have many of these items. Those of you interested in further details should consult Appendix II.

THE ROPE

For walking and scrambling, you will need a forty-five metre length of nine millimetre kernmantel climbing rope. If you intend to use the rope for basic rock climbing as well, it would be better to buy the stronger eleven millimetre kernmantel instead. This type of rope is constructed with an inner core (kern) of nylon fibres which run unbroken for the full length of the rope, surrounded by a plaited nylon sheath (mantel) which holds the whole structure together (Fig. 56).

Like any piece of specialist equipment, you should treat your rope with respect – after all, your life may depend on it. There is very little to do in terms of routine maintenance apart from the occasional wash when it gets dirty. You may laugh, but a dirty rope wears far quicker than a clean one because of the particles of grit trapped in the sheath. The easiest way to wash it is to take it into the shower with you. Avoid using very hot water, and never wash it with detergent.

The best place to store your rope is either under the stairs or in the back of a wardrobe. It needs somewhere cool dark and airy, well away from direct heat and sunlight, where it runs no risk of being contaminated by chemicals.

In terms of general care, avoid treading on the rope, especially on gritty ground (mountain pebbles can be very sharp), and never use it as a tow rope. Nylon has a low melting point, so take care with all forms of heat including cigarettes. Although many people check their ropes for signs of damage or wear before they set out, it is also a good idea to get into the habit of checking it as it runs through your fingers every time you use it.

COILING

Although you may find coiling tedious to begin with, a correctly coiled rope is essential. There is nothing worse than standing on an insecure ledge in worsening weather, trying to undo forty-five metres of knitting.

Hold the rope about a metre from one end and form a series of equal coils, twisting each loop as necessary to ensure that it lies neatly against its neighbour. Each coil should be formed from lengths of rope which are approximately equal to the arm span of the person who is to carry it.

When you have only about a metre of rope left, find the original end and turn it back on itself to form a loop. Wind the remainder of the rope around both this loop and all the coils, pulling each turn fairly tight as you do so, then thread the end through the loop and pull this tight (Fig. 57). Once coiled, the rope can either be placed in your rucksack, or carried over your shoulder.

When you come to use the rope, undo it coil by coil, letting it lie in a loose pile on the ground; if you simply drop it, it is almost

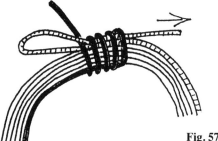

Fig. 57. Tying a coil of rope

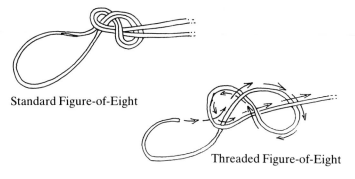

Fig. 58. The Figure-of-Eight knot

certain to become tangled. You should note where both ends lie.
The end which leads underneath the pile is known as the bottom
end, the other as the top end. When using the rope, always pull the
top end first so that it runs out smoothly. If you pull the bottom end
the coils will become tangled.

THE KNOT
Although some books present you with a bewildering array of
knots, many of them are totally unnecessary. You will, no doubt, be
glad to hear that it is possible to utilize a rope safely using only one
knot. However, you will need to know how to tie it in two different
ways, both of which you should be able to do quickly and with a
hundred per cent reliability, with your eyes closed. The knot is
commonly known as the figure-of-eight (Fig. 58).

   The standard figure-of-eight is used to tie simple loops in the
rope, whilst the threaded figure-of-eight is used when you need to
tie a loop around something. Practise tying this knot by both
methods, remembering that you will most likely be cold tired and
wet when you need to tie it for real.

TYING ON

The rope is always worn around the waist. Form a loop by tying a standard figure-of-eight knot, then step into the loop and adjust it so that the rope is tight enough to prevent it from riding up under the armpits, but loose enough to enable you easily to slip your hand beneath it.

ASCENDING DIFFICULT GROUND

It is important you realize that we are not concerned with technical rock climbing in this section. All we are doing is looking at the simplest way in which a rope can be used to give extra security on a scramble or any awkward or steep section of a walk.

Whatever the situation, there is normally a sequence of events which starts with the decision to use the rope. When ascending, the most experienced person ties onto the top end of the rope and carefully climbs the difficult section, choosing a route which heads directly up wherever possible. As he does so, another member of the party makes sure that the rope pays out freely.

Once on easier ground, he makes himself secure (See Static belays) whilst the next person to climb ties on to the bottom end of the rope. The person at the top then pulls in all the spare rope (or slack), so that he can feel the next person, then holds the rope in such a way that he can not only keep it taut at all times, but can also hold the weight in the event of a fall (See Dynamic belays). When, and only when he is satisfied that everything is safe, he shouts down to the next person and tells him to come up.

On reaching the top, and having walked well away from the edge, the second person unties the rope from around his waist and hands it to the original climber, who throws it down for the next person. The sequence then repeats. Note that it is the person who is secure who throws down the rope, not the person who has just climbed. Note also that the person who climbs first holds the rope for all the other members of the party.

Before we continue, you need to know that the term belay can be used either as a verb or a noun. To belay means to hold a rope in such a way that the person attached to it is secure; a belay is a means of securing a person to the rock.

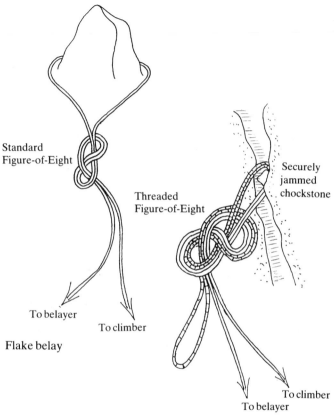

Standard
Figure-of-Eight

Threaded
Figure-of-Eight

Securely
jammed
chockstone

To belayer

To climber

Flake belay

To climber
To belayer

Thread or Chockstone belay

Fig. 59. Static belays

STATIC BELAYS

Before you can safely belay someone over a difficult step, you must
be secured to the ground in some way. This is done by tying the
rope around a convenient chockstone or flake of rock (Fig. 59). If

A thread belay using a figure-of-eight knot.

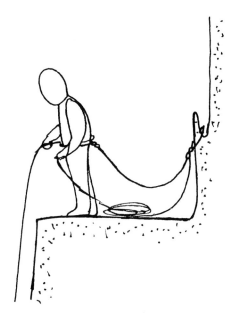

Fig. 60. Back line hazards – No. 1. The line between the belayer and the anchor is so slack he would be pulled over the edge if the climber fell

no suitable anchor point is available, you may be able to construct your own by placing a rock in a crack to form an artificial chockstone. If not, you will have to search elsewhere. The best anchors are those which can resist a pull in any direction.

It is vitally important that you make sure your anchor is safe. Try to move it, kick it, even jump on it (unless this constitutes a hazard); if it moves, find somewhere else. Many people, including some rock climbers, greatly underestimate the forces produced in a fall, and several serious accidents have been caused by the failure of anchors.

It is also important that you realize the anchor constitutes only

Fig. 61. Back line hazards – No. 2. The anchor is so low that the belayer is in an unstable position. Not only could he be pulled off the ledge, but the rope could slip from the anchor

half a static belay; the other half is the stance – the position from which you hold the rope. This should be an area of relatively flat ground on which you can comfortably stand (or sit) and see all (or as much as possible) of the difficult section. Take care not to dislodge any loose stones or rocks.

The relationship between the stance and the anchor is another important factor, and there are three conditions which must be satisfied before the belay can be considered safe.

Firstly, when you are at the stance, the rope between you and the

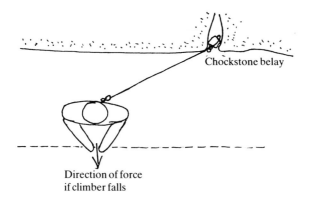

Chockstone belay

Direction of force
if climber falls

Fig. 62. Back line hazards – No. 3. The anchor is so far to one side that the belayer is in an unstable position and could be pulled off the ledge if the climber fell

anchor must be taut. If this is not done, you could be pulled off your stance (Fig. 60).

Secondly, the anchor must be above waist height. If it is low, you may be able to satisfy this condition by sitting down (if you do this, make sure the rope is still taut). If the anchor is below waist height, not only are you potentially unstable, but it could also pull out (Fig. 61).

Thirdly, the rope between you and the anchor must run in the same direction as the force which will act on you if someone falls. If this condition is not satisfied you could be pulled sideways (Fig. 62).

DYNAMIC BELAYS

Anyone using a dynamic belay in a mountain situation should themselves be protected by a static belay. In other words, if you hold the rope, make sure you are secured to an anchor. Although there are exceptions to this rule, you can only learn them through experience.

A dynamic belay is a method of preventing a slip from becoming

The dynamic belay. Note tight back line, anchor above waist height, twist in slack rope, and braced leg on the same side as the active rope. Compare this with the picture opposite.

Lethal belaying practice. Note slack back line, low anchor point, feet together leading to unstable position, twist in active rope, etc. This man should be shot.

a fall. It would be difficult to hold the weight of a person simply by
holding on to the rope with both hands, so the belay method makes
use of the friction created when the rope is wrapped around the
body in a particular way.

Pass the rope over your shoulders so that it runs around your
waist. In one hand you will have the rope going to the person whom
you are protecting, this is known as the live or active rope. In the
other hand you will have the rope going to the pile of coils, this is
known as the dead or slack rope. It is important that you identify
which hand contains which rope, for you must take a twist in the
slack rope, as shown in Fig. 63. On no account take a twist in the
active rope, because if the person you are belaying suddenly
slipped, the force could break your wrist.

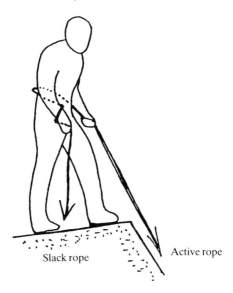

Slack rope   Active rope

Fig. 63. The dynamic belay. Note how the twist is in the 'slack'
hand, and how the 'active' foot is forward and braced. Waistline,
backline and anchor have been omitted for clarity

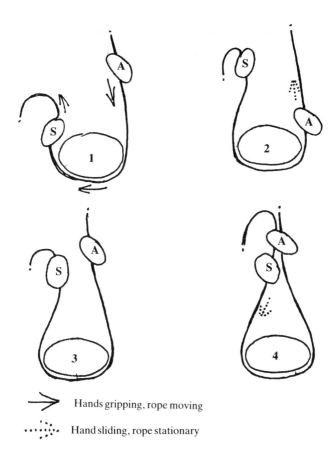

→ Hands gripping, rope moving

⋯⋮⋅ Hand sliding, rope stationary

Fig. 64. Using the dynamic belay. The sequence of events when taking in the rope using a dynamic belay. **S** = slack hand; **A** = active hand

Taking in and paying out the rope from this position requires practice, and it can seem very complicated when you first try it. The basic rule is never to let go of the rope with either hand – you simply feed the rope around your back, sliding it through first one hand, then the other (Fig. 64). If the person you are protecting falls, immediately tighten your grip on the rope and cross your arms.

When using the dynamic belay, always ensure that all the conditions of the static belay are met (i.e. anchor rope tight and in line with direction of fall, anchor above waist height). You must also make sure that the rope around your back does not rub against the rope leading to the anchor – nylon has a low melting point and friction causes heat.

TRAVERSING DIFFICULT GROUND
There are few differences in the sequence used when traversing difficult ground. However, the rope must be passed behind intermediate anchors in order to reduce the possibility of a swing (or pendulum) in the event of a slip (Fig. 65). These intermediate anchors (or running belays) must obviously be secure.

Rope to belayer

Rope to next climber

Fig. 65. Traversing difficult ground. Note how the climber ties on to the middle of the rope so that it can be retrieved ready for the next person to climb. Note also how the climber has replaced the rope behind projections as he passes

The disadvantage of this method is that it effectively halves the length of available rope because you have to get it back to the rest of the party once the first two people have climbed across. The best way to do this is to get each member to tie on in the middle of the rope, and have the second most experienced person pull it back each time (Fig. 65).

Some books recommend using the rope when walking along sharp-edged ridges in windy conditions. In this technique, three or more members of the party may be tied on to the rope at the same time, the idea being that if one person falls, the others will be able to stop him. In practice, this is an *extremely dangerous technique*, for you run the risk that everyone tied to the rope will be pulled over the edge. The only way to lessen this hazard is to jump over the other side of the ridge as soon as the person falls.

DESCENDING DIFFICULT GROUND

When descending difficult ground, the most experienced person must belay from the top. This means he will be the last person to descend.

SAFETY LINE

These belaying techniques can also be used in a number of other situations, for example whenever a safety line is required (See section 4.3).

ABSEILING

In certain situations it may be necessary to descend steep ground which, for one reason or another, is extremely difficult or even impossible to climb down. When this happens, you will have to resort to a technique known as abseiling.

Although abseiling is fast becoming a sport in its own right, bouncing down buildings, from scaffolding towers and over the edges of viaducts, has very little in common with an emergency situation in the mountains.

You should think of an abseil as a slow controlled descent of the rope. As it happens, because you will not have any specialist gear with you, you will have to use the classic abseil – a technique which usually forces people to go very slowly.

The classic abseil. Note the position of the rope around the body and the way the abseiler is leaning well back. Note also that he has turned slightly sideways in order to be able to see where he is going.

For reasons which should be obvious, it is essential that you find a secure anchor. Abseiling is done on a doubled rope, so that when you get to the bottom you can pull one end and retrieve it. In theory, the anchor acts as a pully; in practice it tends to work more like a friction brake, so it is important that you rig the rope with care. Make sure that both ends reach the bottom, and consider what your situation will be once you have retrieved the rope. It is pointless abseiling unless you know you can continue from the bottom.

Once you have rigged the rope and double checked the anchor, stand astride the double rope with your back to the drop, reach down behind you and pass both strands of rope around your right thigh, across your chest, and over your left shoulder. The rope in front of you is held with your left hand (the guiding hand), whilst the rope over your shoulder is pulled across your back and held in the right hand (the controlling hand) (Fig. 66). The amount of friction caused by the rope passing around your body in this way will make it very difficult to move. It can also make it quite painful.

Before you set off, tuck any long hair inside a hat or hood, and make sure there is no loose clothing which could get snarled up. It is advisable to wear gloves.

Now comes the worst part! Walk backwards to the edge of the drop and lean back, holding your weight with your controlling hand. Keep your legs slightly apart (to give you more stability), your knees just fractionally bent, and keep leaning back until your body lies at an angle of between 60° and 90° to the rock (Fig. 66). If you lean too far back you will somersault; if you do not lean back far enough, your feet will slip.

Once you have reached the right angle, you simply walk slowly and sedately backwards down the cliff, placing your feet flat against the rock. Do not try to emulate the commandos or you may bounce the rope away from the anchor.

It cannot be stressed too forceably that abseiling can be extremely dangerous if not done correctly. Unless you are a rock climber or have practised it with a safety rope on several occasions and in different weather conditions, it would be wise to regard it very much as a last resort.

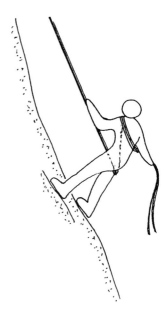

Fig. 66. The classic abseil

WARNING
Good ropework can save lives. However, when done incorrectly, it can also kill. Unless you are a rock climber or have studied, and practised, the techniques in far more depth that I have had space to describe here, use it only as a last resort. As I said at the beginning of this section, the situations requiring its use are all avoidable. You should not have to use a rope unless you want to.

I have made no mention of ropework during winter conditions, for this would take a book in itself. Although dynamic belays will remain the same, static belays may be far more difficult to arrange, as anchor points will often be buried beneath a covering of snow. Whilst it may occasionally be possible to use conventional anchors, different types of snow and ice require different static belays, and you will be forced to take with you a number of extra items. If you wish to read about rope techniques suitable for winter conditions, several books containing relevant information are mentioned in Appendix II. However, simple reading will be insufficient, and I strongly advise you to practice the various technqiues with someone experienced, or to go on a course. Further information on courses can be obtained from several of the organizations listed in Appendix I.

4.8 River crossings

River crossings cannot be regarded as a major hazard in the British mountains. However, accidents occur year after year, mainly because people underestimate the power of water.

A stream in spate is an awesome sight. Not only can it cause severe flooding both in the mountains and in the surrounding lowlands, but also it can roll large boulders along its bed, demolish bridges, fell trees, and move vast quantities of material in suspension. Some streams rise and fall so rapidly that you can literally watch it happen, but even if the changes are slower, your crossing point of the morning may be totally inundated by the afternoon.

Most streams present few problems. If you are on a path, there may well be a bridge; if you are going cross-country, the majority of streams will be narrow enough for you to cross with ease. However, there may come a time when you are faced with a river which is too wide to leap, and in which potential stepping-stones are so widely spaced that they require tricky jumps to reach them. In this situation you should look for an alternative site at which to cross.

In the simplest of terms it is a matter of scale. It is fine to step across the river using rocks, provided you are careful and realize that they may be slippery. If, on the other hand, the rocks are so widely spaced that you have to lunge for them or jump, you would be well advised to find another site.

THE ALTERNATIVES

Never cross a stream at night or when it is in spate. If the water level is well up, you basically have two alternatives: either make a detour to find a bridge or safe crossing point, or wait until the water level drops. Although mountain streams rise and fall with astonishing speed, most people tend to opt for the detour. In this case, make sure you consult your map before you set off; there may be a bridge nearby, or the stream may split into several channels, each of which will be shallower. If you cannot see an obvious crossing from the map, it is best to head upstream for the bed will become narrower in that direction.

CROSSING POINTS

If you are faced with an unavoidable crossing, perhaps the safest of several alternatives, try to read the water in order to find the best place. Avoid crossing at bends, where the water is often deep and fast flowing, and at rapids, where there will be a fair amount of turbulence. It is better to find a wide section where the water is slower and shallower, or where the stream splits into several channels divided by shingle bars or small islands. It is a good idea to look for a viewpoint above the proposed crossing place, for this will often show you such hazards as submerged rocks which you otherwise would not notice.

The best way to learn about water is to stand on a bridge over some rapids with a canoeist, and ask him to point out all the features. Get him to explain stoppers and standing waves, and why water behaves the way it does.

CROSSING PROCEDURES

Once you have made the decision to cross, there are certain things you should do. Firstly, take off your socks, and either roll up your trousers or take them off completely. Not only will this help to reduce drag, but it also means you have dry clothes when you reach the other side. You must, however, wear your boots.

Secondly, close your rucksack as tightly as possible so that air is trapped inside. This will act as buoyancy should you be swept away. However, if you are wearing the sack, this buoyancy will be on your back, and this will push you face down in the water. You must

Rhaeadr Ogwen. Crossing such a stream in spate is an extremely serious undertaking.

therefore undo the waist belt and loosen the shoulder straps before you start to cross, and immediately slip the rucksack from your shoulders should you have problems.

CROSSING TECHNIQUES

One of the best ways to cross is in a huddle formed by three people facing each other and linking arms (Fig. 67). The heaviest person should face upstream. In this method, only one person moves at a time, the other two acting as supports. The most dangerous time is on entering and leaving the water.

If the current is particularly strong, it may be better to move together in a line abreast (Fig. 68) as this offers less resistance to the water. Although some books tell you to do this by holding on to the branch of a tree, it is better to link arms, for in the situation where you are most likely to need it, branches may be at a premium. Using tent poles in this method is extremely dangerous as they so easily come apart.

Whilst it is far better to cross in a small group whenever possible, you may find yourself in a situation where you have to cross by yourself. If this is the case, face upstream presenting a diagonal profile to the river (Fig. 69). If you have a tent pole which can be used as an upstream support, so much the better. Do not be tempted to face downstream as the force of the water may buckle you at the knees.

Whichever method you use to cross, take short shuffling steps,

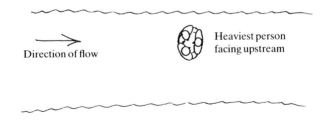

Direction of flow

Heaviest person facing upstream

Fig. 67. River crossing – huddle method. Heads together, arms linked, feet apart. Only one person must move at once

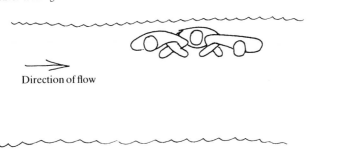

Direction of flow

Fig. 68. River crossing – line abreast

Direction of flow

Fig. 69. River crossing – solo method

making sure each foot is placed securely before moving the next.
Keep your feet apart and resist the temptation to cross your legs as
this can throw you off balance.

EMERGENCY PROCEDURES
If you have misjudged the conditions and find yourself being swept
away, slip your rucksack from your shoulders, hold it across your
chest, and try to get into a position where you are floating feet-first

on your back. In practice, this will not be easy, but you must try, for in this position you may be able to fend off the odd boulder. Do not attempt the impossible by swimming against the force of the current; it is better to go with it taking the occasional stroke to get you near an area of slack water from where you might be able to reach the bank.

USE OF ROPES
Finally, several books mention various methods of crossing streams with ropes. All are extremely dangerous if done incorrectly, for a rope held in tension by the force of water can literally pull you under. The only time I would advise using a rope is where there are steep banks leading down to the river on either side. Fixing a rope across the river may help with the descent and subsequent ascent, and it can also be used as a handline.

Conclusion

This book grew in the writing. As I wrote each section I began to realize that I would have to add bits here and there in order to explain a particular feature or the cause of a hazard. When I read through the first draft I found cross-references that led nowhere and several unexplained conditions. I hope that all these omissions and dead-ends have now been rectified.

However, even now I appreciate that there are things which have not been discussed that some may see as glaring omissions, and the emphasis which I have put on certain aspects of mountaincraft may not be to everyone's liking. Some may criticize me for glossing over what they consider to be essential knowledge, whilst others may say I have gone into irrelevant details. All these criticisms will, of course, be justified, for how can anyone write conclusively about a subject so wide and yet so personal as mountaineering?

What I hope I have done is given you food for thought, and encouraged you to visit the mountains to learn for yourselves. Such skills as ropework and mountaineering first aid can only be learned at first hand, and you are not going to be able to recognize avalanche conditions unless you actually see them. The only way you can possibly hope to learn about mountaincraft is by regularly visiting the mountains and gaining experience in all conditions.

Although I have tried to cover the basics, I may have left out a few things. Should you feel this is the case, or should you have any comments, I would be happy to hear from you so that, in the event of second edition, I can rectify any mistakes.

Appendices

Appendix I Useful organizations and addresses
Such is the popularity of mountain activities nowadays that no matter where you live there is almost certain to be a mountaineering or walking club in your area. Details of these can usually be found in the back of the relevant magazines, or you can write to the representative body:

British Mountaineering Council
Crawford House
Precinct Centre
Booth Street East
Manchester M13 9RZ
Tel. 061-273 5835 (general enquiries and membership)
       061-273 5839 (publications, courses, etc)
       061-272 5163 (insurance, reciprocal rights card)

Details of Scottish clubs can be obtained from the secretary of the Mountaineering Council of Scotland, whose current address can be obtained either from the BMC or from:

Scottish Sports Council
1 St Colme Street
Edinburgh EH3 6AA
Tel. 031-225 8411

If you are interested in more general walking, you might like to contact:

The Ramblers' Association
1–5 Wandsworth Road
London SW8 2LJ
Tel. 01-582 6826

Courses in various aspects of mountaincraft are run at the National
Centres:

Plas-y-Brenin
Capel Curig
Nr Betws-y-Coed
Gwynedd LL24 0ET
Tel. 06904 280 (bookings)
      06904 214 or 363 (offices)

Plas-Menai
Llanfairisgaer
Caernarfon
Gwynedd
Tel. 0248 670964

Glenmore Lodge
Aviemore
Inverness-shire PH22 1QU
Tel. 047-986 276 (bookings)
      047-986 256 (offices)

In addition to these Sports Council centres, the British
Mountaineering Council runs a variety of training courses, and
there are many other excellent organizations which offer holidays
and courses to individuals and groups. Their addresses can be found
in the relevant magazines. The author offers courses in various
aspects of mountaincraft, full details of which are available from:

Kevin Walker Mountain Activities
James Street
Llangynidr
Crickhowell
Powys NP8 1NN
Tel. 0874 730554

Information about the Association of British Mountain Guides can be obtained from their secretary, Alan Hunt, at:

11 Dean Park Crescent
Edinburgh
Tel. 031-332 3468

Appendix II **Further reading**

A visit to any bookshop will show you that there is a wealth of literature about mountain activities. Some books are descriptive, others instructional, whilst many are a mixture of the two. Although this bibliography is far from comprehensive, I have tried to give a representative sample.

Some of the books listed are now out of print, but may be available from second-hand book shops or public libraries.

TECHNIQUES AND TRAINING

Mountaincraft and Leadership, Eric Langmuir, Scottish Sports
    Council/MLTB, Edinburgh, 1984.
Mountaineering, Alan Blackshaw, Penguin, London, 1970.
Mountaineering (The Freedom of the Hills), ed. Peters, The
    Mountaineers, Seattle, 1982.
Mountain Navigation Techniques, Kevin Walker, Constable,
    London, 1986.
Safety on Mountains, British Mountaineering Council, Manchester,
    1975.

WEATHER CONDITIONS

Cloud Study, F. H. Ludlam and R. S. Scorer, Murray, London,
    1957.
Mountain Weather, David Pedgley, Cicerone, Cumbria, 1979.

Mountain Weather for Climbers, David Unwin, Cordee, Leicester, 1978.
Understanding Weather, O. G. Sutton, Penguin, London, 1960.

HUMAN CONDITIONS

First Aid for Hill Walkers, Jane Renouf and Stewart Hulse, Cicerone, Cumbria, 1982.
International Mountain Rescue Handbook, Hamish McInnes, Constable, London, 1984.
Mountaineering First Aid, Lentz, Macdonald, and Carline, The Mountaineers, Seattle, 1985.
Mountain Hypothermia, British Mountaineering Council, Manchester, 1973.
Mountain Rescue and Cave Rescue, Mountain Rescue Organisation, Stockport, 1987.

MOUNTAIN CONDITIONS

Avalanche Enigma, Colin Fraser, Murray, London, 1966.
Avalanche and Snow Safety, Colin Fraser, Murray, London, 1978.
Modern Rope Techniques, Bill March, Cicerone, Cumbria, 1976.
Modern Snow and Ice Techniques, Bill March, Cicerone, Cumbria, 1973.

GENERAL INTEREST

Annapurna, Maurice Herzog, Jonathan Cape, London, 1952.
Classic Walks, Ken Wilson and Richard Gilbert, Diadem, London, 1982.
Conquistadors of the Useless, Lionel Terray, Gollanz (out of print).
Everest the Hard Way, Chris Bonington, Hodder & Stoughton, London, 1976.

High Adventure, Edmund Hillary, Hodder & Stoughton, London, 1955.

History of Mountaineering in The Alps, C. Engel, Allen & Unwin, London, 1971.

I Chose to Climb, Christ Bonington, Gollancz, London, 1969.

Let's Go Climbing, Colin Kirkus, Nelson, 1960.

Mirrors in the Cliffs, Jim Perrin, Diadem, London, 1984.

Mountaincraft, G. W. Young, Methuen, 1949.

Mountaineering in Scotland/Undiscovered Scotland, W. H. Murray, Diadem, London, 1979.

Next Horizon, Chris Bonington, Hodder & Stoughton, London, 1976.

Nothing Venture, Nothing Win, Edmund Hillary, Hodder & Stoughton, London, 1975.

One Man's Mountains, Tom Patey, Gollancz, London, 1971.

On Snow and Rock, Gaston Rebuffat, Kaye, 1963.

Rope Boy, Dennis Gray, Gollanz, London, 1970.

Sacred Summits, Peter Boardman, Hodder & Stoughton, London, 1982.

Scrambles Amongst The Alps, E. Whymper, Ten Speed Press, California, 1981.

South Col, Wilfred Noyce, Heinemann, London, 1954.

Space Beneath My Feet, Gwen Moffat, Hodder & Stoughton, London, 1961.

The Ascent of Everest, J. Hunt, Hodder & Stoughton, London, 1953.

The Complete Mountaineer, George Abraham, Methuen, 1907.

The Games Climbers Play, ed. Ken Wilson, Diadem, London, 1978.

The Shining Mountain, Peter Boardman, Hodder & Stoughton, London, 1987.

The Winding Trail, ed. Roger Smith, Diadem, London, 1981.

Two Star Red, Gwen Moffat, Hodder & Stoughton, London, 1964.

MAGAZINES

The Great Outdoors, Climber, Footloose, Mountain, High (Journal of the BMC) etc.

Many of these magazines carry stories, instructional articles, gear tests and surveys, as well as items of news and gossip. There are also directories of equipment retailers and clubs, and the magazines are excellent sources of information.

GUIDEBOOKS

Most mountain areas in Britain are covered by walking and climbing guidebooks. In addition to those published and distributed by major companies such as Constable, there are several small concerns (e.g. Heritage Guides) who produce guidebooks of both a specialist and general nature.

Many mountaineering clubs produce guides of their local areas. Some of these are professionally produced and distributed nationally, whilst others are little more than special editions of the club newsletter.

Index

Figures in *italics* refer to illustrations or diagrams